THE AUTOMOBILE
GOLD RUSHES

Also by Charles Wallace Miller, Jr.

Stake Your Claim!
The Tale of America's Enduring Mining Law

THE AUTOMOBILE GOLD RUSHES

AND DEPRESSION

ERA MINING

CHARLES WALLACE MILLER, JR.

UNIVERSITY OF IDAHO PRESS
Moscow, Idaho
1998

Copyright © 1998 by Charles Wallace Miller, Jr.
Published by the University of Idaho Press
Moscow, Idaho 83844-1107
Printed in the United States of America

02 01 00 99 98   5 4 3 2 1

LIBRARY OF CONGRESS CATALOGING-IN-PUBLICATION DATA

Miller, Charles Wallace, Jr.
    The Automobile Gold Rushes and Depression Era Mining /
by C.W. Miller, Jr.
        p.   cm.
    Includes bibliographical references and index.
    ISBN 0-89301-195-9 (alk. paper)
        1. Gold industry—United States—History—20th century.
    2. Gold mines and mining—United States—History—20th
    century. 3. Bimetallism—United States—History—20th century.
    4. Gold standard—History—20th century. 5. Depressions—
    1929—United States.   I. Title.
HD9536.U52M53   1998
338.2'741'0973—dc21   97-11450
                                                              CIP

Pencil drawings by Todd Brannan

In Memory of My Parents

Emabel O. Miller (1909–83)
and Charles Wallace Miller, Sr. (1911–83)
Veterans of the Great Depression,
which focused their lives.

Contents

Illustrations

Maps

Tables

Acknowledgments

First and foremost, acknowledgment of the long-term support of my wife, Connie, is in order. She aided in research, diagrams, and typing both for the present volume and for my previous book, *Stake Your Claim! The Tale of America's Enduring Mining Law*.

In addition, the staffs of several fine research facilities were quite helpful. The California State Library at Sacramento provided many of the newspapers and photographs relating to the Far West. Ms. Cathy Correa was outstanding. The Bancroft Collection at the University of California at Berkeley had most of the rest of the materials relating to California. Mr. Bill Roberts made available the papers of Walter W. Bradley, even though they had not yet been completely catalogued. The Arizona Historical Society at Tucson, the Colorado Historical Society at Denver, and the Idaho Historical Society at Boise provided materials related to their respective states, as did the Sharlot Hall Archives in Prescott, Arizona. Last, but certainly not least, great thanks go to the University of Idaho, for providing materials from the library, and to the staff of the University of Idaho Press.

Introduction

Mining in the American West brings to mind the classic picture of a solitary old prospector with his gold pan, followed by a reluctant burro, roaming the remote and rugged western terrain in search of a strike. There is considerable truth to this colorful, romantic image, but there is also truth in similar scenes such as a placer miner working a sluice box or an underground miner mucking (loading) ore from a tunnel floor in a hand-pushed ore cart by the light of a flickering candle. In more recent times, visitors to the western states are struck by the immensity of open-pit mines where enormous trucks that can carry up to 200 tons or entire railroad trains move masses of ore and operate on a huge scale with much greater efficiency.

Which of the above scenes has the greatest historical validity? At what times? Though clearly the independent miner with little capital could participate in a nineteenth-century gold rush, is western mining since then the province only of large businesses? If so, how long has this been the case? Indeed, are the images of lone miners versus huge industrial mining concerns mutually exclusive or have both functioned simultaneously for extended periods of time? And when did the American mining frontier of the individual miner end and a different stage of development begin?

In attempting to answer these questions, I want to refer to the frontier school of historical interpretation espoused primarily by Frederick Jackson Turner in the late nineteenth century and given credence by other respected historians such as Walter Prescott Webb and Ray Allen Billington. Turner's thesis, stated in a celebrated paper he delivered in 1893 entitled "The Significance of the Frontier in American History," noted particular social, political, and economic characteristics that were derived from the presence of vast, relatively undeveloped lands and resources. According to the frontier school, democratic political institutions and the democratic spirit itself spring from the frontier environment, and Canada's and Australia's frontier experiences as well as the frontier experience in the United States, are good examples. Other positive characteristics that evolved from the frontier spirit are egalitarianism, self-reliance, optimism, and economic prosperity derived primarily from the development of new resources. Overall, supporters of the frontier school view the presence of an abundance of free land as providing many opportunities for the little man that may not be available in other geographic or social settings.

However, negative characteristics may also flow from the frontier experience. The presence of vast resources may promote wasteful habits, and examples of the mistreatment of native peoples demonstrate that there may be limits to egalitarianism. As early as the 1920s critics of the frontier school emerged, and debates on the merits of this school of historical interpretation have come and gone over subsequent decades. Though frontier school critics have been relatively quiet since the 1960s, a new contingent of scholars opposed to frontier school interpretations of historical events in the American West has emerged in force in recent years. While following interpretations of history within the frontier school framework, the present writer also takes exception to some of Turner's views. Geography, and the presence of a frontier, naturally create background for human events, but other background conditions may also be significant.

During the Great Depression, the overall economy of the 1930s was the primary background factor, not the presence or absence of a geographic frontier. Even in 1893, Turner himself quoted the report of the director of the U.S. Bureau of the Census that the 1890 survey it had conducted found, with a few remote exceptions, that there was no longer a frontier in the United States in the sense of a progressing line of settlement of areas previously uninhabited by people of European background or ancestry. But even though the government and the academic community had proclaimed the physical end of the frontier by the 1890s, a crucial factor in interpreting historical events within the frontier school framework must address the question of whether or not a psychological frontier remained present as background to historical events.

As I stated in my previous book, *Stake Your Claim! The Tale of*

America's Enduring Mining Law: "The frontier thesis includes a psychological outlook that the West can provide some form of solution to any problem that may emerge. This outlook extends to large-scale national problems as well as individual problems" (p. xi). The psychological application of the frontier school interpretation can be applied throughout U.S. history and to many different contexts, but mining history seems to epitomize the frontier thesis. After all, mineral development is always a kind of frontier, even in developed areas, since ore or underground rock possibilities are simply unknown—a true frontier—until a tunnel, drill, or even a shovel penetrates them.

With this background in mind, some reanalysis of the end of the frontier is in order. Despite the "official" designation of the end of the frontier in 1890, there were many new mining developments of overwhelming importance that continued across the western U.S. after that date. Just as Turner was giving his famous paper in Chicago in 1893, the nation suffered the onset of a severe economic depression which was tantamount to the better-known Depression of the 1930s, though it did not last quite as long. Earlier in the nineteenth century similar economic dislocations had ended in large part due to renewed frontier development. Presumably since the frontier was gone in 1893, it could not help rescue the country from economic upheaval.

The locale immediately to the south of Pikes Peak, Colorado, was not a frontier in the 1890s in the sense of being remote or far from developed areas. Indeed, early stampeders had entered the same area in 1859 but lacked the expertise to recognize the unusual telluride ores present there. In the interim an important mountain resort city, Colorado Springs, had developed nearby. It was not until July 4, 1891, after the official end of the frontier, that Winfield Scott Stratton filed a mining claim which ultimately led to a new major mining region centered at Cripple Creek. Turner had also observed that the mining frontier was different from the agricultural frontier; certainly Cripple Creek constitutes a prime example.

It took several years between Stratton's filing and development of Cripple Creek as a major mining center. However, the additional gold produced by this region by the late 1890s was so substantial that the nation's economy markedly improved, and Cripple Creek provided the main thrust of this recovery. Subsequent gold discoveries in Alaska and Canada's Yukon also increased the money supply, maintaining prosperity into the new century, but these locales still epitomized the remote, undeveloped frontier. Many aspects of the new discoveries at Cripple Creek reflected the same circumstances found in earlier mining frontiers, which had been more remote from developed communities. The lands that ultimately included the mines were unclaimed federal property subject to mining claims under the Mining Law of 1872, and the boomtown municipalities of Cripple Creek, Victor, and several smaller towns achieved a total population of 50,000 in the peak year of 1900. Inhabitants did drift away in subsequent years as production declined, with many participants moving on to Tonopah and Goldfield, Nevada, which became new boomtowns in 1902, further aiding the prosperity of the new century. (The process of recovery of gold by cyanidization which became technically feasible in the 1890s also increased production and boosted the money supply.)

In my view, the mining frontier remained active and significant long after 1890. My approach in the present book is to examine the duration of a frontier element in the industry *and* in the general psychology of the inhabitants of the western United States in order to gain deeper insight into one of the great but relatively little-known periods of mining—the mining rushes of the 1930s.

ONE

Beginnings

As time goes by, fewer and fewer people have a direct experience of what life was like in the 1930s. The contemporary national consciousness continues to rely on a few time-worn images to evoke this era by depicting down-and-out individuals in bread lines and makeshift shantytowns called Hoovervilles or Okies crossing the country in broken-down trucks or men riding the rails looking for work. During this challenging time, many individuals surprisingly found work and a place to live through mining. The Mining Law of 1872 allowed residence on mining claims on federal lands, and even a poor bit of river gravel could marginally support a family and provide a site for a makeshift dwelling. These very small operations accounted for less than three percent of total gold production and were not even listed by the U.S. Bureau of the Census as mining firms. Nevertheless, these marginal operations probably enhanced the psychological states of their owners by making them feel more productive than many other victims of the Great Depression.

Scattered throughout the western states were families who had some background in mining from earlier times, even if they had abandoned the activity in the early twentieth century. Many westerners had roots in a mining heritage because family members had previously worked a mining claim or built a cabin in a mining area, creating an affiliation with the land. Only a few had a legal patent, the grant of full, private ownership that had been created by the government under the Mining Laws of 1870 and 1872 (not to be confused with the patents granted by the government giving protection to inventions). The sons and daughters of old-time miners often returned to family-owned locations, but there were many others who had no background in mining that also came to participate in this activity.

At the beginning of the twentieth century, mines throughout the West had shown good profits when burgeoning industries demanded copper, lead, zinc, and other metals. Gold, the traditional symbol of early western mining, also continued to yield handsome returns. Even silver, in the doldrums in the 1890s, showed some recovery. However, the end of World War I saw a decline in the market for precious metals while rising labor and production costs—which are always detrimental to precious metal production—eroded returns. This pattern continued through the 1920s, a generally inflationary period, and industrial metals were able to remain in demand and profitable while precious metals were not. The early 1930s saw a reversal in this trend. In a deflationary economy, gold became more valuable relative to other commodities, and the value of gold was ensured by the U.S. Mint's policy of automatically purchasing all gold brought to it for $20.67 per ounce; by late 1933 this had climbed to $35.00 an ounce.

At the start of the decade, however, the idea of gold mining seemed to be beyond the realm of the average person. The days of the '49er, the rugged individualist who mined for himself, had been relegated to the history books. But over a relatively brief period, this situation reversed itself and the result can only be described as the automobile gold rushes, the subject of this book.

Indicative of this shift is the following human-interest feature that appeared on February 6, 1930, in the *San Francisco Call Bulletin*, which was typical of similar items that followed during the ensuing years. The *Call Bulletin* had dispatched a reporter, Ashley Turner, to Tuttletown in central California's famous Mother Lode[1] region to investigate several local residents who had made remarkable discoveries. The headline stated, "Children Join Mother Lode Gold Rush." Dorothy Fuller, 14, and brother Buster, 7, were panning on tailings at the foot of an old stamp mill with the permission of the landowner, who also gave them a gold pan. The reporter noted that they had recently lost their father. Their average return was $9 per day, with a one-day record of $17. Two other children, aged 10, had tunneled under the local schoolhouse, where a pocket of $65,000 in gold had been located in the previous century.

Turner also mentioned two individuals who had long experience

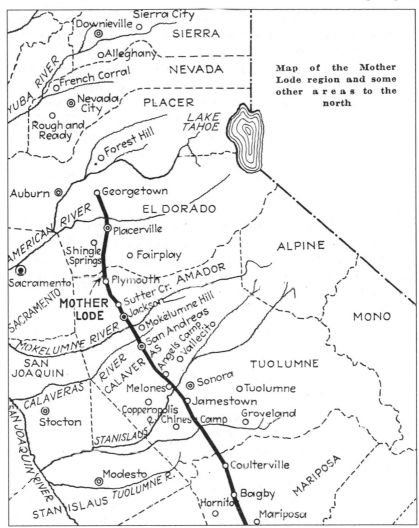

Map 1—*Some maps of California's Mother Lode extend the ore belt farther north in a large arc to include Nevada City and Downieville.* Engineering and Mining Journal *135, no. 11, p. 506 (used by permission of Maclean Hunter Publishing Co.).*

in the region. Charles Gillis was the son of one of Mark Twain's partners from the days when America's most celebrated storyteller was just beginning his writing career in California. By 1930 Gillis was a mature man, and he had opened a new mine on Jackass Hill near

Twain's cabin. Fred Bryan, who was also an experienced miner, found a pocket worth $1,800 and was still celebrating when the reporter filed the story.

Another notable incident in the article involved high school teacher Frank Moyle, who had leased a mining claim for five years from a local store owner. Moyle and his 17-year-old son began to dig a shaft. The father became discouraged when they reached 35 feet but the son kept faith in the venture, and at 50 feet they found a pocket of wire gold which filled two five-gallon oil cans. Subsequently they found a single nugget worth $500 as the grand finale to a total estimated take of $15,000. The neighbors guessed they had much more.

These spectacular quick-money stories were leavened by the reporter's more sober observation that "there is no wild excitement in the Mother Lode. Mining today is for the experienced and mining operations cost money. Yet every man, woman, and child in Tuttletown today is out gold hunting. Mostly they own claims. From grandpa—and grandma—to baby they are gold hunting."

This early story demonstrates that many of the participants were long-term residents of mining areas. They were knowledgeable and positioned to make the most of the renewed value of gold. These activities replicated the great rushes of 1848 and 1849. After James Marshall's initial discovery of gold in January 1848, it was California's own residents who first descended on the Mother Lode region and were able to scoop out the cream of the pristine placer deposits. It took well over a year for news to reach the East and generate the better-known rush of '49ers.

The 1930 story appeared only in California, but at the end of that year another headline, "Autos Speed to New Mines," sowed more public interest throughout the West, even though it discussed lode mining in Nevada, an enterprise far beyond the capability of the typical individual.[2] Overall, mining remained quite depressed, as was the entire nation, and the situation was worsening with the collapse of the market in industrial metal prices.

Against the deepening Depression, various governmental officials began to take notice of the rising potential for renewed gold mining. One of the first individuals in an influential position to do so was California Republican Governor James—Sunny Jim—Rolph. Even though his reputation met with subsequent criticism on several other issues,[3] he showed remarkable foresight regarding mining beginning with his inaugural address. Admitting that he had no personal background in the field, Rolph told the Legislature:

> One of my urgent ambitions as governor will be to accomplish something in the way of stimulating and reviving that languishing industry. I would like to see the entire Mother Lode and all the mining regions humming with activity. . . . The decreased production of new gold is due to nationwide and worldwide economic conditions over which the gold miner himself has no control; and because the price of his product is fixed by government action as the basis of our (and other nations') monetary system, the gold miner is entitled to special consideration at the hands of our lawmaking bodies both of state and nation. . . . California should be in the forefront of the movement to help.[4]

California's original gold rush had also received additional impetus when President James K. Polk encouraged mining in his annual message at the end of 1848. Certainly many of the '49ers would have come West based on news of the strike alone, but Polk's "official" endorsement undoubtedly aided the movement, as did Rolph's speech.

It was unclear from Rolph's speech, however, what direction the renewal of gold mining should take. Was it to be only for the major mining concerns, as his political opponents might suggest? After all, Rolph was a Republican who had been elected in 1930 at the onset of the Depression even though Democrats had won most of the country. Or was it to be a repetition of the individualistic original rush of 1849? As will be seen, the actions of the California State Division of Mines soon encouraged the latter course, however, at this point in time, the worsening Depression was the major news. Very few people, even in the West, had made a connection between gold and possible personal financial improvement.

Professionals in the fields of mining and economics soon added an extra dimension of "official sanction" to Rolph's opinion about mining. As early as February 1931, Adolph Knopf of the U.S. Geological Survey predicted a full-fledged gold rush.[5] *The Engineering and Mining Journal* editorialized in August 1931:

> [Gold mining is] an industry that is immune to Depression—that, in fact, thrives on lower commodity prices; [that] becomes

a favorite subject for mental (and financial) speculation; . . .
[and in which] insufficient gold is the cause of low commodity
prices. Whether sharing this opinion or not, everyone unites in
agreeing that a gold boom at this time would be a definite benefit to industry as a whole.[6]

Others echoed the message in a variety of articles over the next
three years. John W. Finch, director of the U.S. Bureau of Mines,
spoke to the U.S. Chamber of Commerce and summed up with the
succinct comment, "The time to mine gold is in hard times." This
quote became an axiom of the mining industry. By 1931 many participants with little or no prior experience were working claims
throughout the West (see chapter 2). As early as March of that year
the warmer climate near Los Angeles allowed activity in San Fran-
cisquito Canyon. In this small area at least "two score" miners, many
with families and automobiles with full camping gear attempted to
find gold. Most were complete novices at the trade, but a few old-
timers were present and they provided instruction for the rest. One
experienced placer miner reported an average income of $.50 per
day, with one day's recovery at $8.00.[7]

Within another month similar stories were coming from the
Mother Lode. Over fifty were working one stretch of eight miles
along the Yuba River, enough to draw attention in April of 1931, but
nothing compared to what would occur in subsequent years. The reports from this particular area gave no figures regarding profits but
did discuss the miners and their living conditions. One participant
was 80 years old and living in a tent. Another miner, a black man,
had built an eight-by-eight-foot shack but had seen it washed away
in rains and had decided to move on. Families were also present and
all members worked the claims when they could.[8]

These stories of early 1931 reported no spectacular discoveries
but did maintain the "human interest" aspects, as might be expected. Instead of the long-time residents, an influx of small placer
miners with little experience was evident in 1931. Both stories portrayed a more active picture in the Mother Lode compared to the
previous year and demonstrated that the region was changing
markedly, and both stressed the hard work involved in the task of
mining.

One Mother Lode gold buyer reported his average purchase

was only $6 but that he had purchased twice as much as the summer before. The Bank of America, another buyer, reported its purchases up 200 percent. One woman in Amador County panned successfully in her own backyard and even sank a shallow shaft but did not report any figures for her success. The most spectacular single find reported in the spring of 1931 was $25 in gold when one panner found "virgin placer ground" on Hangtown Creek where an old wall had caved in and exposed a pocket. The *Arizona Republic* carried a photo on September 17, 1933, showing a gold ring with three diamonds of one carat each that a California gold panner had discovered. Inside the ring was the date 1853. Another panner discovered a silver dollar in fine condition dated 1795, one of the first coins struck by the new nation, which deserves "honorable mention."[9]

In the spring of 1931, the California Division of Mines found itself crowded with information seekers. At this point the state agency could either provide practical information that would enhance the gold recovery skills of individuals who lacked capital and experience or concentrate on using its resources to the benefit of the scientific and industrial communities. The direction for the agency depended on the director, Walter Bradley, who bore the official title State Mineralogist.

Bradley had held this influential position since 1928 when he was appointed by California's previous Republican administration. Bradley had grown up in San Jose, California, where his father was a locomotive engineer. He graduated from the University of California at Berkeley in 1901 and had been Captain of the Cadet Corps. Subsequently, he worked in various jobs in the western United States and Mexico. After some years of practical experience, he returned to Berkeley to finish a master's degree in engineering in 1917, then acquired more industrial experience before joining the state agency.[10]

Early in Governor "Sunny" Jim Rolph's administration, Bradley expressed concern about maintaining his position, even though he described himself as a "Progressive Republican." A confidant advised him to develop a good relationship with the new governor, and Bradley did just that.[11] Since Rolph had already voiced his desire to encourage mining in his inaugural address and began promoting

Fig. 1— California State Mineralogist Walter W. Bradley.
Courtesy of the California State Library, Sacramento, Calif.

mining in all forms, regardless of how much capital, experience, or
background participants had, Bradley found a secure place in the
new administration and carried out this universal promotion of gold
mining. However, he faced one major drawback in 1931 due to the
seasonal nature of mining. The placer season in the Mother Lode
generally ran from May or June to October, when rains slowed or

ended most activity. The California Division of Mines did not have sufficient time to produce new materials for the 1931 season, but the agency did distribute copies of older guides that had been collecting dust for many years.[12]

The increase in mining in California as early as 1931 was repeated in other locales with historic placer gold production. Many of these places were steeped in frontier mining history. For example, no less a source than the *Engineering and Mining Journal* reported that Deadwood, South Dakota, where "Wild Bill" Hickock had drawn his infamous dead man's poker hand of aces and eights in 1876, was again a boomtown by mid 1931. At the same time, discovery of areas not previously known to contain gold on the San Miguel River in southwestern Colorado and at American Fork, Utah, drew local rushes.[13]

But not all reports were optimistic. After the 1931 season, the *New York Times* ran a discouraging mining story from California:

> these pitiful adventurers set forth full of hope but with no more idea of how to do the trick than a pup has of hatching eggs. Fortunately, they seldom get beyond reach of a filling station. . . but plenty of hopeful miracle seekers are attempting the job this summer.[14]

This reporter neglected to note that the '49ers themselves had no experience and had gone forth expecting to simply pick nuggets from the ground. He also failed to mention the relatively simple skills required for placer mining. He was in a distinct minority in his negative outlook during this initial season and had not realized that major governmental entities would encourage a continuation of mining ventures or that the Depression would deepen and reach its lowest ebb the next year.

The automobile gold rush had gained momentum by 1932, and the modern communications industry began spreading the news across the nation. Sacramento, California, a moderately large city of approximately 125,000 that was the state capital and the gateway to the Mother Lode, paid special attention as conditions developed. In May of 1932, Sacramento newspapers published stories on the increase in the number of miners throughout California. The *Sacramento Bee* reported that "Twin Sisters Locate Twin Gold Mines" near Redding, and that 200 miners at the major mining town of

Grass Valley were engaged in primitive mining using long toms, devices that were about ten feet long which had not been seen for three-quarters of a century. The *Sacramento Union* said that the "State Witnesses 'Gold Rush'; Amateurs Mine," and noted one former department store clerk who was making $35 per day reworking tailings. The paper also mentioned the symbolism of new mining activity near the site of the original monument commemorating the initial 1848 discovery by James Marshall. Even the movie industry showed an interest. On September 18, 1932, the *Arizona Republic* carried an article under the headline "Films to Join in Gold Rush." Warner Brothers used actual placer miners for a scene in the movie *Silver Dollar*, which recreated a nineteenth-century rush. As a result of this type of interest, the Sacramento public library reported a "rush" on available literature on mining.[15]

So what literature was available at this time? In April 1932 the California Division of Mines issued 3,000 copies of a basic "how to mine" manual; all were gone in one week. By 1934 a second edition, which included a lengthy discussion of good locations throughout California, was also sold out within days. Also gone were 8,000 copies of a 25-page summary of this longer work. Official agencies in Idaho, Arizona, Montana, and New Mexico printed similar guidebooks in 1931 and 1932, then updated them as the decade progressed. These publications also disappeared quickly. The Montana School of Mines sent Professor Oscar Dingman to prospect sites along the Missouri River before writing that state's manual. That season an estimated 4,000 would mine this locale. One thousand copies of Dingman's work, State Bulletin No. 5, had sold out in a few days after its publication. A team in New Mexico identified two interesting areas known as the Old Placers, in the Ortiz Mountains south of Santa Fe, and the New Placers, in the San Pedro Mountains. The terms old and new were relative since miners had worked both areas since 1828 and 1839, respectively. Even so the agency officially remarked that both still had potential.[16]

The U.S. Bureau of Mines published circular 6611 that contained basic instructions on how to mine and distributed 7,000 copies in early 1932. By 1934 the authors had revised the booklet five times. This compact volume featured excellent maps of areas with placer potential for all of the United States plus the territory of Alaska.[17]

Privately published guidebooks also did very well since they were often endorsed by professional mining journals. However, the average person with no prior experience or background was more likely to pick up one of the several soft-cover booklets. A comprehensive title, *Gold Placer Mining for the Practical Man*, was published by the Mining Information Service of Denver in 1932 for just $1.00. A very rudimentary pamphlet by Leroy Palmer, Mining Engineer, *Gold Mining—Opportunities and Pitfalls*, sold for a mere $.10.

All through the 1932 mining season, the *Idaho Daily Statesman*, the state's leading newspaper, ran a series of feature articles designed to encourage mining. Idaho State Mine Inspector Stewart Campbell wrote several articles, and the series culminated with retired State Mine Inspector Robert N. Bell's memorable articles offering mining experiences dating back to the 1880s. Historic placer production had been more extensive in Idaho than any other state except California. During the last period of intense gold development between 1911–15, Idaho produced approximately 29,177 ounces of placer gold, which was almost as much as lode production from the state. Colorado was slightly lower, but California produced over a dozen times as much even by that late date. Virtually every Sunday paper included a mining article, usually with historic photographs.[18]

Any of these guidebooks would provide novices with a start in the field. However, those from the California Division of Mines were more detailed regarding the disposition of gold recovered. The various branches of the U.S. Mint all purchased gold but only in lots of two ounces or more (previously they had accepted only lots of five ounces). The miner could sell to the mint in person, by mail, or by express service. In making a sale by mail the miner also had to send a separate letter giving details about where the gold was found. The mint returned payment in three to five days, about $40 for two ounces, either in a check, cash, or gold coin or bars prior to 1933, as the miner requested.[19] (After 1933 gold coin and bars were all called in by the government as part of Roosevelt's policies, as discussed in chapter 3.)

The miner could avoid the licensed buyer's fee if he could accumulate the required two ounces to take or send to the mint. During the 1930s the government operated three facilities that were mints (i.e., they manufactured coinage) in San Francisco, Denver, and Philadelphia. However, federal assay offices could also purchase gold at the same prices with the two-ounce minimum. A mint at Carson City, Nevada, had closed in the 1890s but an assay office still functioned there. The other assay offices were at Helena, Montana, Boise, Idaho, and Salt Lake City, Utah. (An incident in August 1932 outside the Salt Lake City assay office created a minor stir. Two miners in town after several weeks in the diggings were carrying their gold pans and the gold they had recovered, worth $82, in a bottle. Just as they were about to enter the assay office, they dropped the bottle in the street, spilling the gold, but they soon recovered it by panning in the gutter!²⁰)

George Cantini was from a family that had mined in the Mother Lode for generations. By the mid 1930s, when Cantini was age 10, his immediate family was living in Sacramento but still drove back to the Mother Lode to work some of their own placer claims on weekends. In an interview with the author, he recalled that they had kept a cupboard full of receipts for gold sales to the mint for many years, but unfortunately these have been lost.²¹

However, most of the small-scale placer operators worked on such a narrow margin that they simply could not wait to accumulate two ounces required by the mints. They invariably needed cash and they also had the option of selling to private buyers licensed by the mint. In 1932 there were 70 private buyers in California, and a scattering in other states. A story of July 24, 1932, in the *Arizona Republic*, entitled "Survey Shows 10,000 Persons Working Coast Gold Streams," with a dateline of San Francisco, stated that the licensed gold buyer with the largest shipment to the mint was a Chinese storekeeper named Ching Wing, who had shipped $1,200 monthly since spring 1932; the second largest was the Bank of America branch at Oroville, California, with $1,100 shipped over the same period. Two years later, there were over 200 licensed buyers in California alone. Most of the licensed buyers were owners of small stores and other businesses in mining regions, though all branches of the Bank of America, as well as some other banks, were also buyers. A licensed buyer was completely free to pay what he wanted, which was always somewhat less than the mint, but he would often give a break if the miner was purchasing from his store.²²

Two gold buyers even merited separate human interest stories. The first was Chinese-born Charley Yue who had run a store in the Mother Lode town of Auburn, California, for many years. Though a licensed buyer, he had not made any purchases for so long that he had forgotten that he owned a pair of scales. By mid 1932 he had found them and was using them daily. Significantly, he paid $16 per ounce, the same figure that a number of other licensed buyers quoted. The second was Roy Davenport, who stated that virtually every transaction at his hardware store at the town of John Day, Oregon, required a measure of gold. By mid 1932 few customers even approached him with outright currency.[23]

A variety of observers are known to have made field inspections as the movement was developing. In the early spring of 1932, three old-timers, V. A. Harpoole, George Hawksworth, and Andy Moore, decided to make a 125-mile wilderness trek through areas of historic activity in Montana. They had personally hiked through the same areas in the late nineteenth century but had seen only abandoned workings. These old-timers figured that their knowledge and the remoteness of the locations gave them an advantage in finding a profitable spot. They were quite surprised to discover that every cabin along Snowshoe Gulch was already occupied. Some 50 to 60 families were present; all but two families were from Elliston and Maryville, Montana. The newcomers were averaging $2 to as much as $8 per day.[24]

In June and July of 1932 State Mineralogist Walter Bradley made an extended tour of the Mother Lode and subsequently made shorter tours of that area and other gold locales in California. He met literally hundreds of participants and dutifully logged the numbers working at each site. He also spoke to gold buyers, local bankers, and larger operators and recorded his contacts in a series of notebooks. Bradley gave estimates compiled only from the licensed buyers that he met of 4,645 to 4,973 participants in mining but did not note if those were actual miners or entire families. Between Bangor and LaPorte he personally counted 1,400. Approximately 100 were working on Mariposa Creek near the mouth of the Fresno River; William Krohn, a local businessman, had grubstaked 75 of them.

Aside from lode mines, the most spectacular find Bradley recorded was one nugget of 1½ ounces by a father and son near Sonora. One miner near Downieville had done poorly but said he would sell two gold crowns from his mouth if he needed food. On the Cosumas River Bradley saw ten men working, some using an

Alaska Jack box, a device with two removable trays that worked like a double gold pan. At Plumas, in the northern end of the Mother Lode, the miners had a gentlemen's agreement allowing each man 60 to 100 feet along Rush Creek. The typical licensed buyer had 20 to 30 regular gold suppliers but each reported many more people in their respective locales. At LaPorte a buyer named Maxwell estimated his purchases at $2,000 per month in gold. The best recovery Bradley recorded was an average of $1.00 per day with $.40 to $.50 being typical.[25]

Subsequently, he published the highlights of his tours in a remarkably poignant article in the highly technical *Engineering and Mining Journal*. This excerpt portrays the sentiment of the entire account:

> The camps of these gold seekers are pitched beside the roads, on the river banks, and even perched on scanty footing on steep gulch sides. Some have tents; others are without. Yet with all the struggle and hardship of it, I found not one grumbler among the scores interviewed. All seemed smiling and happy to be in the great outdoors, with its independence, though the actual gold harvest might be scanty. They have at least reduced the numbers in the bread lines in the cities during the past three summers [1932, 1933, and 1934].[26]

Bradley's remarks are most revealing since he was a professional mining specialist, not just a news reporter who briefly visited areas of activity and sent off a story. George Cantini stated from his memory of the period as a child that this description was quite accurate.

Similar comments by the *Leadville Herald Democrat* (Colorado) in mid 1932 are also insightful. This particular paper had a long history in a region known for both placer and lode mining. The editorialist rhetorically asked: "What is actually being accomplished by the army of fledgling placer miners who have been induced to go into the gulches and pan for gold?" The answer was "nothing practical." However, he obviously believed the psychological benefits were great since he continued the passage, "For some of the Argonauts the adventure in the wilds may be a real benefit if they do not become charges on the communities." The editorialist admitted he was more optimistic than Dr. M. F. Coolbaugh, President of the Colorado School of Mines, who foresaw problems if people came from other states to placer mine, failed, and stayed on relief in Colorado. Coolbaugh lauded the value of professional exploration that was on-going during the automobile gold rush.[27]

At the same time, the *Idaho Daily Statesman* took an editorial position more optimistic than the *Leadville Herald Democrat*, even though it was strongly Republican in political orientation. The *Statesman* noted that many decades of mining activity had reduced the potential of finding a big bonanza, but such events were still possible, even in placer mining. It encouraged activity along the Salmon River, which loops through the mountainous regions of central Idaho where lode gold is prevalent and washed downhill to the river. However, historically production along the Snake did not suggest much potential for gold recovery in the 1930s. Some 300 miles of the Snake was relatively accessible and had long seen mining activity, as attested to by literally hundreds of pieces of abandoned equipment. Virtually anyone could see colors of very fine gold by panning along the Snake and Boise Rivers, and coarser particles could occasionally be found after spring floods, but profitability was another matter.[28]

The Spanish word *placer* simply means shallow. It connotes mining in sand or gravel beds in or near streams where rivers have carried gold particles from vein sources at higher elevations. Placer gold particles can be very fine but nuggets may form as smaller particles accrete to each other as materials move downstream. The laws of physics determine good locations for deposition of placer gold, such as along the inside of a meander or bend in a stream.[29]

The typical placer miners of the early 1930s generally had no capital and had to make do with the most basic equipment. In this respect they were very similar to the original '49ers of the previous century. However, despite the Depression, the automobile gold rushers were definitely more fortunate than their counterparts of an earlier time. First, they did not have to cross great distances of wilderness, jungle, or ocean, a process which literally killed as many as a quarter of those who started for California in the mid-nineteenth century. Instead, they could drive to the diggings in a matter of hours if they were already in the West or days if they were in the East.[30] Second, many of them had some rudimentary knowledge of placer mining and its techniques *or* could gain it quickly either from those more knowledgeable or from special courses or from legitimate guide books.

The general lack of wherewithal was the most serious problem even to those willing to put forth considerable physical effort. Observers who visited the placer areas commented that the equipment resembled similar pieces from the past century. According to Walter W. Bradley, "One sees the simple pan, rocker and long tom, or short, single sluice boxes with an almost indescribable variety of riffles and screen, burlap, or matting bottoms, and newfangled devices, both patented and homemade, some with considerable merit and efficiency; others with less."[31]

Publications from Bradley's own agency, beginning with the 1932 pamphlets, described these devices and emphasized that even novices could construct and use them. In placer mining all processes depend on the weight of gold, which allowed it to remain behind while some agitation method removed lighter materials. Pure gold has a specific gravity of 19.3 (compared to water at 1.0), though most nuggets have some content of silver and other materials that lower the average to about 16. Yet that weight is still far more than most gravel materials of quartz or feldspar, which typically have a specific gravity of 2 to 3.5.

The gold pan is usually made of steel and is a little more than a foot in diameter and about three inches deep. The miner fills it with a shovelful of river gravel and water. After tilting the pan slightly and moving the pan in a circular direction, the miner removes the largest chunks and discards them. Presumably any gold adhering to these pieces has washed off and remains in the pan. The panner repeats the process several times, continually removing gravel in descending size, and carefully pouring out a little water each time. Ultimately, the pan is left with heavier minerals with a specific gravity greater than 5.2 (mostly black grains of magnetite), and hopefully particles of gold. Over an eight-hour day, a skilled panner could process perhaps nine cubic feet of materials or 1/3 of a cubic yard (27 cubic feet). Both these units of measure are used throughout the subsequent discussion.[32]

Trade publications took note of the return of basic equipment. The fact that no gold pans were available in western Montana by the summer of 1931 was sufficient to draw a full editorial. (Presumably miners could use frying pans as substitutes, as many had done in the previous century.) One Montana hardware store alone had sold 800. Indeed, gold pans were still in short supply as late as the fall of 1933.

Hardware dealers as far from the Mother Lode as Los Angeles first sold out their old stock of pans, which had accumulated 15 years of dust since prior activity. Even after the initial period of interest, they could not keep new pans—which sold for about 65 cents each—in stock.[33]

As shown by several cases mentioned earlier, some miners attempted to recover larger amounts than simple panning could provide, but frequently had little more capital than the individual restricted to a pan. With basic carpentry and a few planks, even a poor miner could construct rockers and sluice boxes, the same equipment that the '49ers had used. A rocker (or cradle) was still small-scale equipment. It consisted of a wooden device which truly appeared to be a baby's cradle. Gravel poured in a screen box or hopper would fall down an inclined board called an apron and finally settle along riffles on the bottom. The heavier gold collected behind the riffles. The miner literally rocked the entire device while working two to four cubic yards of material per day.

The sluice box was the next step up in capacity. The sluice box was 6 to 10 inches high and 10 to 14 inches across and consisted of an inclined trough with riffles on the bottom. Miners simply shoveled gravel into the upper end of the trough and allowed a flow of water to carry the materials down its length, sometimes as much as 50 feet but usually shorter. Gold, if present, collected behind the riffles. The longer the box, the finer the gold it could collect. Even particles as fine as those found on Idaho's Snake River could be collected in an extended device known as a woolen burlap table machine, which was essentially a *very* long sluice box.

Often miners placed mercury behind the riffles to chemically "catch" the gold. (Mercury is one of the few chemical elements or compounds that adheres to gold and can thus be used to attract small particles.) A large sluice had a capacity of as much as 300 cubic yards in a 24-hour period. Several miners were needed if they were using ordinary hand shovels, though those who could afford a loader or other power earthmoving devices could make up for the labor of a number of shovelers. A long tom was simply a variation of a sluice box but usually a little shorter and built in one movable section. A dip box was not as long, but was positioned at a very high angle with a covering screen to separate out the larger materials before they even entered the device. This variation needed less water. None of

Fig. 2—A dip box in California's Mother Lode in 1932. Saturday Evening Post, *Oct. 10, 1932, p. 10.*

these pieces of equipment required more than a few hours' practice to successfully learn how to operate. Those who used very small methods and frequently moved from place to place often bore the name "snipers."[34]

Of course even simple equipment required some skill and knowledge to successfully operate. One account reveals some interesting problems. An amateur group working near Butte, Montana, on historic German Gulch went so far as to copy the design for a rocker from an exhibit at the Montana School of Mines. However, they recovered nothing. When they approached a professor at the school he identified the problem. The amateurs had used an old oil can to pour water into the device. Oil, or even greasy human skin, can make gold too slick to catch in simple devices. Old-timers knew this fact but amateurs had to learn it the hard way to be successful.[35]

By mid 1932 the automobile gold rush was well-known in the western United States and to the mining community in general. The relationship to the then current economy was inescapable. The chief of Idaho's mining agency stated, "There are probably hundreds of men occupied. . . . Every digger becomes one less candidate for a job on the outside. Most of them are scratching for ground that the old timers overlooked." Walter Bradley made similar observations in a speech in Los Angeles and guessed that 15,000 people were actively mining, but other contemporary estimates for 1932 ran as high as 25,000 at any one time; many of these were women and children.[36] The figures of 15,000 to 25,000 or more accounted for workers only and did not count families, which made the total populations of the placer regions much larger. The magnitude of the automobile gold rush is even more remarkable considering the official U.S. Census report of only 37 placer gold mines, which employed 686 people throughout the U.S., as recently as 1929. (That same year over 50,000 were working in western mines that produced industrial metals, primarily copper.)[37]

In 1932 more human interest stories about the automobile gold rush appeared in newspapers. The *San Francisco Chronicle* reported another incident of children finding gold in a shaft they dug in their backyard in Sonora, California, and an "aged prospector" who lived in a San Francisco hotel drew a story because he was looking for a partner to help him return to the trade.[38]

Stories of two spectacular discoveries at Grass Valley and Tuttletown, California, spread farther than most of the earlier finds when they went out on the Associated Press news wire. At Tuttletown a miner identified as Bob Newmeyer found a single nugget worth $1,300. Though some discoveries as early as 1930 in the same area had been equally spectacular, they did not get the publicity that Newmeyer's strike did.[39]

There is little question that Newmeyer's find and the national attention it received contributed considerably to furthering the velocity of the automobile gold rush. When college student Bill Powers received nationwide publicity for the $3,000 in gold he recovered in Idaho at the end of the placer season of 1932, he proved the Idaho State Mine Inspector wrong. Just a month before the Inspector had dismissed the summer work by college students as being relatively trivial compared to professional prospectors. As with Bob Newmeyer, discoverers of spectacular placer bonanzas frequently found them in areas not previously worked and at some depth below a layer of gravel or other barren materials.[40]

The success stories of various individual discoveries are associated with classic rushes across the West in the previous century. The best-known include James Marshall at Sutter's Fort, California, in

Fig. 3—Bob Newmeyer's success was the most publicized of any individual during the Automobile Gold Rush. He is pictured here holding his $1,700 nugget and smaller pieces from his strike on Jackass Hill. Saturday Evening Post, *Oct. 15, 1932, p. 11.*

1848, Henry Comstock in 1859 in Nevada, Ed Schieffelin at Tombstone, Arizona, in 1877, H. A. W. Tabor at Leadville, Colorado, the same year, and Winfield S. Stratton at Cripple Creek, Colorado, in 1891. All of these figures were significant enough to move into the history books. The equivalent figures for the initial automobile gold rushes were clearly Bob Newmeyer and Bill Powers but neither is well-known in mining history, just as the entire automobile gold rush has been overlooked as well.

A step up in national attention came when the *Saturday Evening*

Post dispatched Arthur H. Carhart to make extended field observations in Colorado in the summer of 1932 and sent Samuel G. Blythe to California's Mother Lode. Both of their articles appeared that fall.[41]

In Colorado Carhart logged 550 miles on "roadways threading through Fairplay, Alma, Breckenridge, Dillon, Kokomo, Leadville, and a dozen other old camps that are flushed with the touch of gold fever." He interviewed miners on Cherry Creek within the city of Denver, where some of the original discoveries had started rushes back in 1858 and 1859. In 1932 the scene was similar, but gold panners now found themselves working only a short distance away from the autos which were whirring by on Speer Avenue, which today is still one of Denver's major thoroughfares.

Carhart reported that many placer areas had been worked and reworked for decades. After all, "gold does not grow like crops," but stream flow can naturally replenish slight amounts in a worked-out area. Occasionally miners still found pockets of good gold-bearing gravel. One old-timer summed up the entire process by stating, "Can't make [a day's] wages just panning. We're goin' to the hills next week to work a placer lease on shares. It's good ground an' we'll probably make wages there usin' a sluice."

Carhart also went to more remote areas to report on larger scale activity. One classic lode (or vein) mining area is high in a mountain range around Fairplay, Alma, and Breckenridge, near the very center of the state. As early as the 1860s, miners dug portals literally on the tops of mountain peaks over 14,000 feet high, then tunneled back inside the mountains. (In 1991 I climbed two of these peaks, Lincoln and Bross, and inspected these historic workings, which are clearly marked on topographic maps.) Over geologic time a considerable mass of gold flowed downstream in rivers from this range and naturally spread out in all directions from the mountains. The gold collected in large gravel areas as the streams lost intensity in locations where they entered more level ground. Carhart was in the middle of this region when he wrote:

> A motley procession of autos followed the roads to the gold camps. Many had out-of-state licenses and often displayed gold pans and shovels among brimming bundles of duffel. Along the road between Fairplay and Alma were dozens of tents, and

> near by men worked sluices and hand rockers. . . . Along the
> road were slab-walled shacks, log cabins, and tents—abodes of
> camp followers of the gold army. Today's stampedes in the
> Rockies may be by automobile but they do not lack in other ac-
> couterments of the gold boom, even to claim jumping, a gun
> fight or two, and rough walled palaces of chance.

The local economy showed considerable increase in property values
and even considerable permanent construction, a most remarkable
situation considering that it was 1932.

Carhart reported that all previous gold rushes had soon seen "go
homers"—those who had little luck or just lacked the resolve to stick
with it. He predicted the same pattern would soon prevail in Colorado, especially among the more marginal participants. He seemed
impressed by the occasional "bonanza" stories, citing one case
where six men gophered a shallow hole and found a "haywire mine."
For just 6 sacks, each 80 to 100 pounds, they received $6,000 from
the smelter.

People of all racial and national backgrounds profited from the
Colorado mines. Carhart reported participants of Hispanic ancestry,
and the remarkable "haywire mine" was on a claim owned by a black
man. These classic mining tales prompted Carhart to state, "If history repeats, present activity is the prologue to events of considerable importance; the man with the gold pan and crude cradle is the
actor who pulls back the curtain on a play of greater significance."[42]

The *Saturday Evening Post's* other reporter, Samuel G. Blythe,
was not quite as taken by the mining spirit. However, he found a
number of individual stories in California which were just as enter-
taining as those recounted by his colleague in Colorado. Blythe visited Jackass Hill where Mark Twain himself had mined and where
the famous author had written his first published work of fiction, the
well-known short story, "The Notorious Jumping Frog of Calaveras
County." Less than 100 yards from Twain's cabin, dozens of men
worked in August heat of 110 degrees. "There were camps all about,
with women and children in them, each camp with an automobile of
sorts alongside."

The automobile gold rush brought about renewed interest in the
Frog Jumping Contest, which had lapsed for many years. The *Ari-
zona Republic* of May 20, 1934, noted its return in an article entitled
"Angels Camp Holding Fete." The annual contest has continued

Fig. 4—A typical sluice box as seen by reporter Arthur H. Carhart on his 1932 tour of Colorado. Saturday Evening Post, *Sept. 17, 1932, p. 21.*

since then and has attracted TV coverage, including a slot on the Johnny Carson show.

Regarding the circumstances of earliest evidence of the rush, Blythe wrote:

> The date is uncertain, but some man who had an automobile but no job and no prospects of getting one, and who did not fancy a bread line existence, piled his family into his car in 1931. I have seen small cars with man, wife and 6 or 7 children, with more tucked in [in] the way of tents, bedding, stoves, and so on. . . . They came from all parts of the country but mostly from the Rocky Mountain States, where mining is more or less familiar to everybody. They were still coming in August [1932], when I spent the greater part of a week up along the Mother Lode, mostly in cars—some in fairly good cars; many in cars that barely wheezed along and had terrible times getting up the mountain roads . . . cars of all the cheaper makes, loaded to the roof and above, on the running boards, on the fenders and bumpers with all sorts of gear and with children—hundreds of children—all eager, enthusiastic, ready to make their fortunes and confident they would. . . . No mining technicalities such as claims and so on, bother them. They squat wherever they

please and go to work. . . . Their spirits are excellent. They are
a friendly, helpful lot. Each assists the other. And they are all
very proud that they are making some money, be it 50 cents a
day or two dollars, and not living on a dole.[43]

Carhart and Blythe offered more detailed pictures of two areas in
the West than are available for other locales, but the conditions were
much the same in other gold-producing communities. Near the
town of Baker in eastern Oregon, for example, streams were
crowded with panners. All available housing in the area was occupied, mostly by newcomers whose automobiles bore license plates
from California or the State of Washington. Oregon, though not
generally known for mining, appears to have had more small placer
participation at this time than any state except California. As late as
June of 1934, an unidentified man was credited with recovering
$17,000 near the town of Bend in central Oregon, promoting a rush
of over 1,000 there.[44] In the June 17, 1934, *Arizona Republic*, an article entitled "Started Panning and Struck" described a young Oregon couple, Mr. and Mrs. Robert Burns, who had traveled from
Oklahoma the year before and found a huge nugget in the Old
Stovepipe Mine near Grant's Pass, Oregon. They were pictured with
their nugget, valued at $1,015, nestled in a gold pan.

The fact that the families simply "squatted" without worrying
about "technicalities such as claims" reveals these operations were
transient and some streambeds overworked. Under federal mining
laws of 1870 and 1872, private parties could still remove all valuable
materials from public lands without any fees or royalties to the government, so the marginal placer miners did not need a mining claim
to mine on federal lands since the mining laws designated much of
public domain as "free and open" to mining. However, a mining claim
did have legal value if a party had something of relatively high value:
the filing of a mining claim legally protected against rival miners. The
parties could even purchase placer lands for $2.50 per acre in the
patent process. Many of the placer areas were already private property, having been acquired years earlier from the government under
the patent process. If not fully patented, they were still protected under mining claims which parties kept current with only minimal work.

Certainly, parties with mining experience could and did maintain
property rights over areas with more potential. One woman who
owned a claim in a pristine area drew a 20 percent royalty on all gold

taken. Another party called in authorities to run off 200 prospective claimants (or claim jumpers) at a new discovery on private property surrounded by national forest near Lake Tahoe, California.[45]

However, those who legitimately owned claims often leased them cheaply, especially since there had been little activity for 20 years or more. Sharlot Hall, a prominent figure in Arizona society and politics, received a letter from Mr. Wyatt Smith, who had obviously known her and her family, dated December 1, 1941. Smith, who supported three sons on a placer mine at Jacksonville, Oregon, said:

> Well, the old dredge is here and will soon be tearing into the ground. And my mining days will be over on this place. I have been taking out some mill gold by hand.
>
> I have been prospecting some and found some rich ground. It is under lease to a dredging co. If they can't dredge it, I can lease it. It will run about 10 to $12.00 per yard. There is a outfit here that wants to send me to Payson [Arizona] and take over the Golden Wonder Mine. . . . I have a report on the property. I told them I would leave here soon as the dredge was through. (Sharlot Hall Archives, Prescott, Ariz., Sharlot Hall Collection, item 14, File Folder 3, Doc. Box 4)

As this letter points out, owners of mining claims allowed smaller miners to work the claims by hand until they could negotiate with a larger firm to bring in heavy equipment.

Indeed, the owners of claims of little value sometimes simply looked the other way, considering the poverty of the people mining there and the paucity of their equipment. The owners knew that large machinery could still recover values even after the automobile rushers had skimmed small volumes of low grade materials.

Those who arrived by automobile beginning in 1931 were following a pattern well-known in the West. In the prior century the initial rushes of American, European, and Latin American miners had depleted many of the same areas within a few years. These other groups had excluded the Chinese while the deposits were still easily recoverable, but after they moved on the Chinese miners frugally worked the same locations for additional years or even decades. They did so without claims. Though even the Chinese had moved on long before the 1930s, the automobile gold rushers essentially just picked up where the Chinese had left off.

*Fig. 5—Participants in an adult class in placer gold mining in the Denver area,
c. 1932. Courtesy Colorado Historical Society, Denver, Colo.*

E. J. Webster, another who visited the gold fields, sent a story to
the *New York Times* in mid 1932 which stated

> a rather remarkable revival of optimism [is evident] in Arizona.
> Just why is hard to explain on actual conditions. Not only does
> the spirit of the old-time, ever hopeful prospector prevail, but
> there are an increasing number who are earning a fair living
> from placer mining . . . [with] a recent invention whereby the
> present day miner can handle from 6 to 12 times the quantity of
> pay dirt that was possible with pick and pan . . . miners, often
> tenderfeet, are making $3 to $15 a day.

He went on to describe a course in placer mining offered by the
University of Arizona for "older men and women."[46]

The idea of classes to teach placer mining began to spread all
across the West with the automobile gold rush. During the 1930s,
public assistance programs were the responsibility of state and local
governments, which paid what they could. The city of Denver made
more of its placer deposits, relatively meager as they were, than
most local entities. A city agency organized a program in 1932 which

Fig. 6—An experienced miner instructs an enthusiastic student in basic pan-ning in one of the placer mining courses in the Denver area, c. 1932. Many women participated in the automobile gold rush, in contrast to the nineteenth century rushes when almost all miners were single male adventurers. Courtesy Colorado Historical Society, Denver, Colo.

trained the jobless to placer mine at a site in the city limits on the South Platte River using 40 sluice boxes. Denver's South and West High Schools also organized classes in placer mining which included talks by Frank E. Shepherd, superintendent of the U.S. Mint. Some 90 seniors at Colorado Agricultural College (now Colorado State University) enrolled in the high school placer mining course.[47]

Other cities and organizations began similar ventures. In Spokane, Washington, 1,900 participated in courses over several weeks, and Washington State University and the University of Idaho teamed up to conduct the classes. "The Northwest Mining Association of Spokane, Washington, sponsored a course at the headwaters of the Palouse River in the Idaho panhandle. About 2,000 people attended and saw demonstrations of gold panning and lectures about placer gold given by geological and mining faculty of the Idaho School of Mines. The Association held several additional courses around Washington State and estimated that 5,000 people attended." And in Canada, Alberta's Department of Mines followed U.S. examples by officially sponsoring a camp for 200 unemployed men on the Saskatchewan River (*Arizona Republic*, June 11, 1933).

The city of Boise, Idaho, offered a class by veteran miner George C. Stearns which met in the city council chambers, but with 300 students present, only a few could even see his demonstrations. Here, as at Denver, students could learn in streams within the city limits. As late as 1940, long after the automobile gold rush had peaked, the various New Deal agencies, including the Works Projects Administration (WPA), would adopt training courses as well. Another state that provided adult courses was Montana. Professor Oscar A. Dingman of the School of Mines taught 150 in historic Last Chance Gulch near Helena and over 600 at Great Falls on the Missouri River. Overall, some 50 camps were active in the state, mostly along the Missouri.[48]

The mining town of Prescott, Arizona, made an important local contribution to relief efforts. An association that held 160 acres of placer claims allowed men on the unemployment rolls to keep whatever they could individually recover from the claims. The Yavapai County Road Department provided shovels and picks while the City of Prescott and the Chamber of Commerce provided pans and constructed cradle rockers at $4 each. A "practical placer miner," John Fulton, managed the enterprise with funds through the local Welfare Board. The first 107 shifts produced gold valued at $54 for an average of $.50 per shift. This rate of return was better than some but was still low enough to prompt calls for federal grubstaking and backing. At the time, at least a number of people were working.[49]

The city of San Diego, California, developed a project similar to the one at Prescott in late 1932. However, San Diego's plan was mandatory. Local authorities sent all panhandlers out to work on the city's placer lands in Imperial County if they did not leave town voluntarily.[50]

By the end of 1932 it was evident that a major social, economic, and even historical process was in full bloom. While there may be a minor controversy as to the time of the start of the automobile gold rush, there is no question that it was quite apparent by the second year. Walter W. Bradley's personal inspection in mid 1932 left no doubt as to the size of the movement. Aside from the basic economic conditions and the federal policy of buying all gold presented at the U.S. Mint, Bradley and his agency had probably done the most to stimulate the rush. In addition to many press releases and speeches which Bradley made over the years, he spoke on a number of radio programs in the West,[51] and continually encouraged the automobile gold rush. In later years when gold activity was tapering off, he reflected on the activities of his agency in the frenzied early period:

> For the amateur miners and prospectors who crowded the offices, class instruction in panning and the use of rocker, sluice box, etc. was given in the Laboratory in the Ferry Bldg. [agency headquarters in San Francisco], and in the three years 1931, 2, and 3, between 3,000 and 4,000 persons were so helped. . . . Upwards of 200 persons per day, each in the San Francisco and Los Angeles offices and around 10 per day average in the Sacramento and Redding offices have been given interviews and assisted with information on . . . where to go, what to do, practical prospecting help, geological data, roads and water information, how and where valid mining locations may be made, what is acceptable as assessment work, and many other practical items. An average of around 6,000 samples per year are tested and identified in the Laboratory for the prospectors in the hills, telling them what they have and if it has any commercial value.

Bradley also described the availability of literature from his agency and noted that his staff answered 1,000 letters per month.[52]

Agencies in other states performed similar activities. John Finch, for example, stated that as Dean of the School of Mines at the University of Idaho, he had received 3,500 requests for information from people in the field between 1931 and 1932.[53] But California was far and away the most important simply because it had more miners attempting to begin gold production than all other states combined. There is no question that much of the early impetus for the automobile gold rush was provided by state governmental entities in the West. The federal government would take a more prominent role in the recovery of large-scale mining later in the decade.

Amateurs

The automobile gold rush was still on the upswing in 1933, and in 1934 activity was so intense that this was unquestionably the peak year. However, there was less national interest in gold rush stories, possibly because the event had become old news by that time. Discovery of gold at Grass Valley, California, by crews digging a municipal swimming pool was still of regional interest, but there was no nationwide coverage.[1] Franklin D. Roosevelt and the New Deal had become the focus of national media interest and this distracted attention from the automobile gold rush. Even though the media showed less interest, more and more amateur miners were entering placer areas.

New York Times reporter Tom White wrote from California in June of 1933 that 200 families per day were entering the Mother Lode. Many of these patiently drove several hundred additional miles simply looking for a good, unoccupied site. He predicted a total of 25,000 participants that summer. White inspected the living quarters and conditions of many families in the area and described their foods, which were cooked in Dutch ovens over open fires, as generally adequate and wholesome. Most families seem to "make do as well as when they had a refrigerator, gas range, and radio." He described a typical campsite and other dwellings:

> A canvas awning was spread between the tent and the jacked up automobile. When it rains, this protected space serves as the living-dining room. The car with a cutaway front seat, provides comfortable sleeping quarters. . . . Cabins and shacks, unoccupied for decades, whose ancient roofs have long ago collapsed, have [with repairs] responded nobly to the needs of the miner of 1933.[2]

Of course, many people throughout the country were living in similar conditions, but most of them had less immediate reason for optimism than those in the gold fields. At San Gabriel Canyon in the Mother Lode, one group of 200 called their settlement Hooverville or Hoover Flats, just as residents of many shantytowns on the outskirts of cities did, but there was a major difference. Here the residents lived in a national forest and were at least trying to produce an income. But problems did crop up. The Forest Service estimated that all the camps along the San Gabriel had a total population of 1,000, which was creating sanitary and fire hazards, but no serious incident had occurred.[3]

The poorest of the 1930s placer miners were similar to the Joads, the semi-fictional Oklahoma family of John Steinbeck's classic novel *The Grapes of Wrath* (1940), which later became a famous movie. Steinbeck's Joads were a composite of many families that he personally met, and their experiences epitomized many aspects of the times. Their tragic odyssey included a stint in California's fruit orchards under conditions very near to outright slavery. Other haunting images of Okie culture in California had appeared in the mass media even before *The Grapes of Wrath*, primarily in the unforgettable black and white images taken by photographer Dorothea Lange on a tour in 1938.

Some of Steinbeck's images of the migration and subsequent life were clearly overstated for literary reasons. For example, ordinarily it took only three or four days to travel from Oklahoma to Los Angeles or the San Joaquin Valley, following U.S. Route 66 all the way. Some newcomers did experience serious difficulties in transit but the vast majority arrived without incident. They usually camped along the road, and continued to live in tents for months or even years after reaching California. Many migrants, even Okies, did, in fact, find reasonable jobs, depending on educational levels, skills, etc.

This displacement of farmers due to drought formed one of the larger internal mass migrations in U.S. history. According to the U.S. Census, persons born in Oklahoma, Texas, Missouri, and Arkansas constituted 10.8 percent of California's total population by 1940, or 745,943 individuals, a marked increase from 7.6 percent of the state's population in 1930. After World War II brought new industries to California, the migrants, and their children, became generally just as well off as the overall population.

But the 1930s had been especially difficult for all newcomers to California, with those originating in Oklahoma, Texas, Arkansas, and Missouri faring worse than most others. Native Californians showed surprising prejudice against migrants. Famous reformer Upton Sinclair lost the governor's race in 1934 because of ads he placed against the Okies. Steinbeck would have been equally justified in giving the Joad family some time in the placer areas as well. In fact, one camp bore the local name Oklahoma since its residents were mostly from that state, which had become a dust bowl and had been hit hard by the Depression. Many families of similar circumstances appear to have rotated through a variety of locales in California and elsewhere, but the powerful oppression that the Joads experienced was lacking in the placer mines. The participants could come and go as they pleased and could immediately possess any gold they recovered, meager as it was.

A healthy adult male could shovel perhaps 10 cubic yards of material per day into a typical sluice box. Those 10 cubic yards could bring perhaps a tenth of an ounce of gold or about $2.00 per day in the early 1930s, a figure which increased to $3.50 per day when Roosevelt raised the price of gold from $20.67 to $35.00 an ounce in early 1934. More realistic, though, was a return of $.25 per day, usually from gravel that had been thoroughly worked and reworked.[4]

The following list reflects prices typically found in Colorado and California's Mother Lode region. Prices in Idaho and Arizona were a few cents lower as late as 1934 since these regions had productive local agriculture and competitive retail markets. Of course, advertised items were usually cheaper than unadvertised items and often reflected fruits and vegetables that were "in season."[5]

16 oz. wrapped loaf of bread	$.05–6
4 lbs. bananas	.25
3 lbs. ground beef	.25
1 lb. prime rib roast	.25
1 lb. ham	.25
1 qt. peanut butter	.46
1 pkg. shredded wheat	.11
3 cans peas	.37

3 cans Campbell's soup	.25
1 can tomatoes	.15
1 dz. ears fresh corn	.25
1 dz. eggs	.23
1 lb. butter	.30
1 lb. can coffee	.28
9 lbs. new potatoes	.25
10 lbs. sugar	.62
10 bars of soap	.32
1 pkg. Jello	.05

For storing groceries which needed cooling, a Frigidaire electric refrigerator ran $117.50; an old-style ice box was only $19.95. A combination easy chair and sofa of Angora ran as low as $58.88. A large table-model Philco radio in a heavy wooden case was $22.90. An iron for pressing clothes was $4.95. A tailored men's suit ran $22.50, men's oxford shoes were $4.95 to $7.95, sports shirts $.88, and women's hosiery $.49.[6]

For life in a campsite, a 7-foot by 7-foot, fully enclosed "water-proofed, weather cloth auto tent" ran $7.95, while a three-sided tent designed to fit against an automobile was $4.98. Camp stoves were $4.45. Army cots were $2.47, and a more permanent camp bed ran $6.45.[7]

These prices may seem ridiculously low to a reader of the 1990s, but for many victims of the Depression it was difficult to purchase even the basic necessities. When compared to prices in 1929, the above figures were about half that of the last year of prosperity, showing the magnitude of deflation.[8]

In early 1933, California Governor Rolph, on the advice of State Mineralogist Walter Bradley, proposed sending as many as 300,000 workers to the placer mines using a state or federal program to grubstake this army of prospective miners with tents, trucks, and tools. After Rolph passed away in June 1934, Bradley stayed on as state mineralogist through the 1930s and periodically expressed similar ideas. He was not alone; Democratic candidates for state offices during the Depression echoed Bradley time after time, despite the fact that he was a Republican.[9] A massive program specifically for placer miners never materialized, but New Deal agencies did aid miners in other ways, as discussed in the next chapter.[10]

Many grandiose schemes to employ "armies" of placer miners simply overlooked a number of practical considerations that limited potential. Even though placer materials were generally found along the natural watercourses that carried them from source areas, the lack of water could pose a problem. Sometimes local conditions required pumping. One interesting small operation in Colorado near the famous town of Telluride purchased an antique horse-drawn fire engine that the Denver fire department had kept in good working order. It adequately served to pump water to a sluice. An operation in Idaho had examined a 1903 pumper still owned by the Boise Fire Dept. for similar use, however, the pumper's fuel requirement of 500 pounds of coal per day was unfeasible at the remote location on the Snake River and the venture was abandoned.[11]

In far western Arizona and adjacent desert regions of California, placer gold was present in a number of places where there was no reliable water source nearby. Even though the Colorado River runs through the region and supported placer rushes in the 1860s, farther from the river water was in very short supply in the harsh desert environment. Streams flowed very briefly and quite violently only during the hottest months of the year, and it was difficult for miners to work in the searing desert heat. Even so, human ingenuity made some use of these deposits in the 1930s, especially in Yuma County around the town of Quartzite in southwest Arizona and in Mojave County in northwest Arizona around Oatman and Kingman.

Publications demonstrating the use of dry washers or dry jigs for recovery of placer gold had been available since at least 1912, but had largely been forgotten in the 1920s when placer mining was in the doldrums. During the Depression a number of successful operations revived these methods, which used wind instead of water to separate lighter materials from the heavier gold particles. Dry washers consist of a screened hopper and feedbox and an inclined tray with cross riffles and a cloth bottom. Beneath these parts is a bellows. Two men generally operate the device, one working the bellows while the other fills the hopper and examines the materials, which move by gravity down the inclined tray. Some operators placed small amounts of mercury behind the riffles, just as was done

Fig. 7—A dry placer device used in 1932 in Arizona. Engineering and Mining Journal *133, no. 7, p. 381 (used by permission of Maclean Hunter Publishing Co.).*

in conventional water placer equipment. One inventive individual used an electric fan instead of a bellows to separate the lighter materials, then panned the residue with what little water was available.[12]

Unfortunately, overall gold recovery is substantially less with dry placers, and these locales were among the last to return to production during the automobile gold rush. Further, there is a tendency to lose nugget-sized gold since dry recovery methods work best for grain-sized materials, and several cases are known of nuggets thrown out with the waste. Dry placer devices could process only two or three cubic yards per day. It is no wonder that an official guidebook published by the Arizona Bureau of Mines went so far as to recommend use of water placer methods by "hook or crook" whenever possible. Many deposits in the region would have been quite valuable had a water supply been available.[13]

An individual operator in Mojave County, Arizona, A. E. Lewis, proved this point by recovering $1,000 in the fall of 1933, or $10 per

Fig. 8—A portable homemade sluice which used what little water was available in the southwestern deserts of Arizona. Engineering and Mining Journal *133, no. 7, p. 381 (used by permission of Maclean Hunter Publishing Co.).*

day—clearly a substantial sum—by pumping water from a well over a half mile away. Even though water certainly made a big difference, a number of families still survived using only dry washers during the Depression.[14]

By 1933 small business ventures began entering placer mining. Numerous western firms that had been involved in municipal construction of roads and sewers prior to the Depression had equipment and capital and could pay fees to lease mining claims or private lands. Observers began to notice that the quality of automobiles entering placer areas improved somewhat by 1933 when more business-oriented parties arrived. But as with the original Depression miners, most moved on after finding little of value. When they did operate, though, each could employ a few workers for $3.50 to $4.00 per day. George Cantini remembered that operations of this scale in the Mother Lode were often called "doodlebugging," which implied the use of a mechanical shovel or dragline.[15]

For placer miners with capital, the 1930s presented a much

greater variety of equipment than was available at any previous time. Within a year or so after the start of the automobile gold rush, industrial concerns stepped in to meet the demand for improved recovery machinery. Firms that had traditionally supplied the mining industry with equipment naturally entered the field, and manufacturing firms that specialized in farm machinery also began producing portable placer recovery equipment. To the uninitiated, some of this machinery may have appeared to be Rube Goldberg contraptions. In fact, much of the equipment made a significant difference in the amounts of gold recovered, which positively impacted small business profit margins.

Firms advertised in mining magazines and their machines generally fitted the description of mechanical sluices (which use an engine to move the devices which "catch" the gold). By 1933 two firms in the Midwest were producing large models. The Diamond Iron Works of Minneapolis manufactured a machine which required two gasoline motors of 40 and 15 horsepower to operate, and the *Engineering and Mining Journal* reported several Diamond units working profitably in the Black Hills of South Dakota. The Iowa Manufacturing Co. of Cedar Rapids produced a similar model called the Cedar Rapids Placer Machine.[16]

At the same time, two firms in Denver long associated with mining developed their own versions. The Mine and Smelter Supply Co. presented a model which boasted a capacity of 2½ cubic yards per hour and used less water than equivalent designs by other manufacturers. A smaller model required only one gallon of gasoline per hour to process one ton of materials. This unit cost $209.50. The Denver Equipment Co. produced the Denver Gold Placer Unit for $480. Of course, shrewd bargaining with a dealer could probably bring a discount, and bargaining was part of life in the 1930s. Used equipment was available and subject to even more horse-trading deals than new machinery.[17]

By comparison, the manufacturers' advertised prices for new cars in popular magazines during 1932, 1933, and 1934 listed a six-cylinder Chevrolet as low as $445; a Plymouth thrift two-door sedan ran $495; a new Ford V-8 was $515; a straight eight Pontiac with a 115-inch wheelbase and a weight of 3,265 pounds ran $585; and a new Buick was $795. To provide a frame of reference with the highly prosperous mid 1920s, a Chevrolet ran $525 and a Buick was over

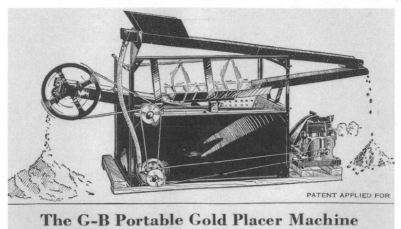

The G-B Portable Gold Placer Machine

Fig. 9—An advertisement for a G-B Portable Gold Placer Machine, a mechanical gold sorter that purportedly could recover finer materials than more primitive equipment. Mines 22, no. 6 (1932), p. 31.

$1,000 just before the Depression hit. The degree of deflation is evident. For those who had even less means, in the early 1930s a typical used car from model year 1927 or 1928 cost $150 to $250 while a workable used car from 1924 or 1925 could be as little as $50.[18]

Gasoline prices were highly impacted by freight costs in the 1930s, which could add as much as 40 percent to refinery prices. Further, there were differences in taxes in various jurisdictions. In oil-producing areas like Texas or Oklahoma, gasoline at retail could run as low as $.10 per gallon. In the Rocky Mountain States a price of $.20 per gallon was typical. The retailer only received about $.02 profit. In mid 1932 a disruption in Texas and Oklahoma caused prices to go as high as $.25, but they soon drifted back down.[19] These figures give an idea of the investment and operating costs required for entry into the placer gold business.

In time the Denver Equipment Co. proved the most successful all-around supplier judging by the length of time it has continued to manufacture implements while other competitors gave up. Their Denver Gold Saver became the generic term for an entire type of gold recovery product, just as Coke became a generic term for cola soft drinks or Xerox became the standard term for copy machines. By 1934 another firm, the Mining Equipment Sales Co. of Los An-

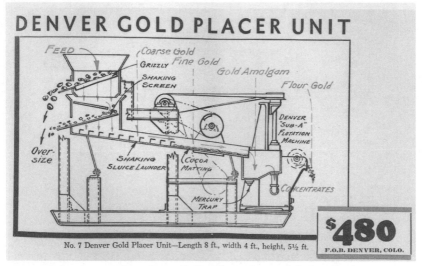

Fig. 10—*This is an early version of what became one of the best-known mechanical gold separators. It became popularly known as the Denver Gold Saver. Mines, 22, no. 5 (1932), p. 31.*

geles, had introduced a different type of device that resembled a small cement mixer—the Hamilton-Gold King machine—which could process as much as 120 cubic yards per day. It used a revolving trommel screen and a 30-inch by 14-inch scrubbing chamber that spun at 50 rpm to sort the gold. Similar models soon became common in the West.[20]

Those with modest capital could purchase still another type of device which expanded recovery capability—the suction dredge. The operator used a hose on what was essentially a large vacuum cleaner to remove materials off a stream bottom. Again, the weight of gold separated it from other materials inside the part of the device which corresponded to the waste container of a regular vacuum cleaner. Some models floated on a type of raft while others rested on a bank. The miner could still move some distance away from the machinery by using a long hose. The suction dredge made it easier to obtain gold from a stream bottom some distance from a stream bank. However, it was not too popular in the early part of the decade, though a rather large floating model was available from the Production Engineering Co. of Spokane, Washington. Later in the 1930s, though,

Fig. 11—The portable G-B Placer Machine offered a smaller version of the mechanical sorter featured in Fig. 10. The advertisement states that it is ideally suited "for testing placer ground or for one-man operations." Both machines were produced by the Mine and Smelter Supply Co. of Denver, Colo., with offices in Salt Lake City, Utah, and El Paso, Texas. Mines 23, no. 3 (1933), p. 23.

suction dredges caught on when smaller models became available.[21]

Walter Bradley claimed that he could "fill many volumes" from the interviews he had with miners, but he only published a tantalizing few and many of these seem to have been taken from memory since they do no appear in his notebooks. One of Bradley's incidents revealed the overall economic importance of the gold trade. A licensed buyer, whom Bradley described as "a big, broad shouldered

Italian storekeeper in the Mother Lode country," dealt frequently in very small amounts of gold. One man brought "jes a litta sonting" in a bottle and requested an exchange for a loaf of bread and some sugar. The storekeeper said, "I weigh heem up. He's 27 c. So I give heem a loaf of bread, some sugar, some rice, and a litta bit of cheese. He go away happy." Another storekeeper reported that his minimum trade had been $1.50, the maximum $25.10.

There is no escaping the fact that small amounts of gold could be directly transferred into a circulating currency in general stores for the basic necessities of life. The '49ers had been able to do the same, but the miners of lode gold had to send their product to a smelter first. True, Roosevelt issued regulations on the private possession of gold in April 1933. Parties could legally mine gold but had to sell to the U.S. Mint or to licensed buyers who then sold to the mint. However, circulation of small amounts was impossible to police, and they had an immediate benefit in the overall economy.

The last incident Bradley mentions reveals an important personal characteristic shared by many participants in the automobile gold rush. A licensed buyer supervised a commercial gravel plant in Fresno County, and when a young man appeared with $3 worth of gold that he had worked for a week to recover from the nearby San Joaquin River and stated that he had a wife and baby, the buyer offered the young miner three days' work at $4 per day. The miner thought it over, then said, "No, thank you. I'll go back to my diggins." Bradley believed that the young man made this decision because "he preferred the independence of being his own boss out in the open spaces, and, of course, there was always the lure that tomorrow he might find a nugget." This individual case represents the overall psychology of the frontier school of historical interpretation that was still active in many of the participants in the "grassroots" history of the western United States. Gold rushes, even in the 1930s, had and have a distinct psychological effect, including extreme optimism as well as independence and self-reliance.[22]

In early 1933 no less a figure than the director of the U.S. Bureau of Mines, Charles W. Wright, candidly admitted that he could only make a guess that 50,000 placer miners had been working in the field the previous summer. He placed the average take at $.30 per day.[23] Since the director of the U.S. Bureau of Mines himself could only guess at the numbers of placer miners, that agency joined with the new Works Projects Administration (WPA) for a special study in 1935, just after the WPA organized. The WPA was a very broad ranging agency with the objective of promoting "work" for all Americans, as its very name stated. It created literally millions of "make work" jobs of its own and also issued a series of reports on potential employment in a host of fields, including mining.

A research team went to the placer regions, focusing on California, but spending some time in other areas. Field interviews and observations continued until 1937. The team missed the peak years of 1933 and 1934, but even so, they published a useful preliminary report in 1937 and a most valuable final report in 1940.[24] The final report is surely the most detailed, intimate contemporary observation of the entire automobile gold rush.

The research team estimated that "at least 100,000" had "tried their hands" at gold recovery in 1933, twice as many as the director of the Bureau of Mines had estimated for the previous year. By 1937 some 22,000 were still at it. These figures represented workers only; with families included, the populations in placer areas would have had to have been much greater. Of all those who arrived, fully three-fourths moved on within two months. Therefore only 1 in 20 who attempted placer mining actually made a living at it and were considered full-time workers, spending 181 working days or eight months per year in the mines. The average take in California was $6.02 per week. The automobile gold rush benefitted most those who were between other jobs and those who had pensions or other income sources.[25]

In California at least 200,000 participated as workers at some time in the 1930s. The U.S. Census of 1930 counted two million male inhabitants over age 21 in the state. Thus at least one-tenth of the adult males in the state participated in the automobile gold rush. In California in 1933 as many as 100 men were working on streams per mile of gold-bearing gravel; by the end of the survey only one or two were present.[26]

It is interesting to compare the number of participants with those of the original gold rush of 1848–49. The few surviving records of local mining laws written for the earliest mining districts allowed claims of "30 by 40 feet," or "ten yards . . . extending to the middle of the river." Other sources state that some locales initially allowed claim sizes only as large as a man could swing his shovel in a circle.

With these distributions, an observer in 1849 theoretically could have counted from 132 to 176 miners working along each mile of river, though often those figures would have doubled where claims went to the middle of the stream. The physical appearance of the Mother Lode in 1933, with placer miners working diligently for mile after mile, was similar to the same region in 1849. By 1933, though, many automobiles were parked along roads that paralleled the rivers.[27]

The team briefly cited a few of the spectacular newspaper stories, noting especially the success of children. They determined that such stories were unrealistic and often did not differentiate between placer mining, which the ordinary person could accomplish, and lode mining, which was highly technical.[28]

The team presented some of its most revealing data using records provided to the U.S. Mint by the licensed gold buyers. Every time a buyer purchased gold, the mint required that the name of the seller be recorded along with the weight and the location with property ownership status. This basic information provided only enough comparative data to allow the researchers to include figures for the smallest sellers who did not own or lease mining claims. The total numbers of sellers often represented larger numbers in families or partnerships; often only one person actually sold the gold. Unfortunately the majority of participants never sold any gold at all, so comparative data are not fully representative.[29]

According to mint records, the number of individuals who made small sales to licensed buyers in 1935 were:

State	No. of Sellers
California	19,463
Oregon	3,229
Idaho	1,314
Arizona	1,184
Colorado	1,047
Montana	711
Washington	250
New Mexico	233

South Dakota	214
S. Appalachians	168
Nevada	130
Utah	41
Wyoming	38
TOTAL	28,022

The team did not report figures for Alaska, which had no through highway from the more populous states to the south until World War II. Hence Alaska, with only 60,000 permanent residents, did not participate in the amateur stage of 1930s gold development. However, simple mathematics reveals the West Coast to have had 82 percent of the total, with 70 percent in the single state of California.[30]

The records supplied to the U.S. Mint by the licensed buyers also allowed preparation of Table 1 for California alone.

Generally miners made two to three sales per year for an average of $72, if they made any sales at all. Many participants simply did not recover enough to sell directly to the mint, though they may have sold to licensed buyers. In 1933 and 1934, the team determined unequivocally that more people were in the mining areas than in other years but many stayed only short periods. By 1935 and 1936 a more experienced, serious cadre of miners was left, and they were mining for longer periods.[31]

Some additional figures on the sizes of gold sales reveal local activity. Unquestionably, the most famous area within the Mother Lode was Calaveras County. In 1935 the U.S. Mint recorded purchases of 200 lots of gold of less than 10 ounces. Further, there were 791 small sales to licensed buyers. By comparison, in 1849 the typical miner in Calaveras County recovered three to five ounces per day on claims as small as 30 by 40 feet.[32]

Similar figures are available from the superintendent of the Boise Assay Office for the year June 1, 1931, to May 31, 1932. All the gold sellers from the Boise Basin numbered 305. They made a total of 536 sales; 172 for less than $50 and 133 for amounts of $50 to $100. Significantly, all 305 were otherwise unemployed. The fact that the minimum sale had been lowered from five to two ounces just before this period was of obvious significance to small miners.[33]

The WPA research team arrived at a number of generalized conclusions that agree with accounts of other contemporaries. They observed "self-reliance, independence, and initiative." Most miners had automobiles but paid little for services which they could do themselves. Most participants appeared to be in excellent health, and there was little evidence of alcohol abuse, though a few were seen to enjoy "short sprees."

However, the transient nature of the experience placed severe strains on family life, schooling, and community involvement. Training from local, state, and WPA programs was valuable but experienced miners undoubtedly gave the best practical lessons and were the key to most successes among newcomers.[34]

The team noted that many individuals had often had problems with employers. The fact that here "no employer was needed" helped provide an overall "salutary psychological effect." They summed up the situation with the memorable sentence, "Miners who stay at the creeks represent the survival of the most successful

Table 1. Small Miners' Gold Sales in California, 1929–37

Year	No. of Small Miners	Total No. of Sales Sold	Total Ounces
1929	43	101	108.84
1930	491	929	955.41
1931	2,497	5,332	6,530.62
1932	12,000	30,880	23,870.00
1933	14,800	38,801	17,312.21
1934	17,649	51,844	23,290.41
1935	19,463	49,193	29,516.95
1936	13,529	35,831	22,984.10
1937	12,422	32,931	15,491.05
Totals:	*92,894*	*245,842*	*140,059.59*

SOURCE: Charles White Merrill, Charles O. Henderson, and O. E. Kiessling, *Small Scale Placer Mines as a Source of Gold Employment and Livelihood in 1935, Report E2* (Philadelphia: U.S. Works Projects Administration, May 1937), p. 109.

and the luckiest men, as well as the most unfit; they form a somewhat unusual agglomeration of personality types." Many had a
"planless" life, while others showed much more focus by obtaining
small power outfits, which required at least $50 in savings. Finally,
the team noted the same striking relation among workers at placer
mines and those who harvested fruit and crops as other observers
had noted earlier.[35]

Miners could also be local nuisances. Some camps were notori-
ously filthy, while others were very clean. The WPA report specifically attributed clean camps to the presence of women. Those on
U.S. Forest Service lands had to follow regulations which protected
scenic values along roadways. Miners had to locate some distance
from roads, though they could still live on mining claims. Often they
ignored hunting and fishing laws because they needed food. Indeed,
the author interviewed one miner who *still* wished to remain anony-
mous since he had violated game laws. Yet they could also be assets
to local communities as well, most frequently by trading at country
stores or by being available to harvest crops, lumber jack, or fight
fires as the seasons required.[36]

The researchers presented a detailed questionnaire with 21 major items to any miners who were willing to respond. Summarized
briefly the questions were: the age and background of the miners;
whether they owned automobiles; how long they had been mining;
time spent mining per week and year; residence at mine or nearby
town; income per day and season; number of dependents; agree-
ments with property owners; and the methods and equipment
used.[37]

The results suggested a division into three different groupings.
Casual miners participated only 30 days or less per year; intermittent miners annually worked for periods between 31 and 180 days;
full-time miners worked for 181 or more days. Note that these
groupings by time worked are different from other groupings cited
in the same report based on gold sales or ownership of claims.[38]

The researchers found that full-time miners were grossly over
represented when compared to the total numbers of people involved in the overall automobile gold rush. The full-time miners
were present at more permanent locations and could be easily identified. Also, in later years the survey gave less opportunity to interview those who had been in the placer areas for relatively brief

periods. Several of the questions focused on California, though the team apparently used the same form in all areas.

In the end the team presented only four generalized conclusions regarding intermittent and casual miners, though they did give details of particular cases from these groups. First, they concluded that intermittent miners were more likely to be relatively youthful and to have families present than full-time miners. Second, intermittent miners were more likely to be between jobs, especially fruit and crop harvesting work. Third, intermittent miners more often had dust-bowl origins. Last, casual miners were more likely to be on public relief, as were intermittent miners, than were full-time miners.[39]

Regarding full-time miners, the researchers based their general conclusions on 204 responses to the questionnaire. Of the 204, some 194 respondents were then residing in California; 147 had been in the state in 1930, though most had migrated from elsewhere, which was true of California's overall population. Of newcomers since 1930, 21 had specifically come to mine gold. Regarding prior knowledge of placer mining, 56 had experience before 1929, some 13 had experience before 1900, and one had experience dating back to 1875.[40]

Of the full-time miners, 76 percent were over age 40 and 49 percent were over 50. Of the 204 interviewed, 139 had no dependents while 65 had one or more. One hundred and forty-one owned or had part ownership of automobiles, but these were described as ancient vehicles with an average age of 10 years or more. Only one used a packtrain of burros. One third of the total owned power equipment which required an investment of at least $50 and often considerably more.[41]

Only 102 answered the question regarding status of lands worked. Of these, 63 worked with permission on claims or private property owned by other parties with no obligation while eight paid a royalty. Twenty-four owned their own claims. One hundred and eighty-two responded to questions regarding dwellings. Of these, 73 lived in tents, 63 in cabins, 23 in "shacks," 6 in houses, 4 in trailers, 3 in autos, and 10 in no particular dwelling.[42]

One hundred and eighty-five gave estimates of the hours they worked. The median was seven hours; however, many people worked six or even seven days per week since they often lived in remote areas and there was little else to do. Income on a yearly basis for full-time placer miners was $260.[43]

The final report included a number of brief points of interest selected from the questionnaire responses. Beginning with casual miners, two "fruit tramps" ages 39 and 59, who were partners, placer mined off season. Another man rotated between work in the fruit industry and placer mining; he had been a coal miner in Illinois. A group of four, ages 53, 67, 22, and 17, were joint owners of an automobile and were making $.35 per day on the Feather River in California. A woman, age 40, received some income from the lease of a farm she owned; she also made $.05 per day placer mining about four hours. Three "old-timers" on the Stanislaus River, ages 68, 69, and 74, had many years of mining experience. A father and son, ages 43 and 20, had come from Nebraska to placer mine. Four brothers ranging in age from 54 to 60 had their own claim and cabin in Siskiyou County, California. They had placered in Montana in 1933 and had worked in the California harvest.

A husband, age 44, his wife, and 2-year old son had come from Pennsylvania where the husband had been an electrician. He drew a monthly pension of $70 as a disabled World War I veteran. Another family lived in an "improved dwelling" built on a truck frame. They had also rotated with the California harvest. They were from the state of Washington where they owned a farm, for which they received $125 per month, but planned to return.[44]

The group defined as intermittent miners most frequently rotated between placer mining and agriculture in season. Several examples from the data are illustrative. A former carpenter, age 56, was spending more of his time prospecting for "hardrock" veins. The caretaker of a small estate, age 56, also placered part-time. He worked one yard of gravel per day through a sluice box and put in an eight-hour week. Two "old-timers," ages 65 and 61, had placer mined since 1895 and 1896. An out-of-work cook estimated that he was making $1.00 per day. A group of four shared a tent and shack. They were still working for the WPA as well, but expected to be laid off soon.

A miner, age 39, on the American River traveled between placer grounds and crop areas in an old model car. A former sign painter from Minnesota, age 59, could only spend five hours per day mining since he was also working for the WPA. A former chauffeur, age 33, averaged $1.00 per day over a 100-day season. A former lineman, age 29, supported his parents on $1.50 per day. A hardrock miner, age 28, worked a small vein as well as placer mining. A former electrician on the Boulder (Hoover) Dam project, with no age given, also placered while prospecting for lode gold.

A former machinist, age 52, built his own two h.p. dredge. He made $300 to $400 per season over four months working just three hours per day. A miner in Mariposa County, California, age 28, intermittently worked for $125 at about $1 per day when he placer mined. A man who also sharpened tools lived in his car and drew a pension of $35 per month as a Spanish-American War veteran. A former hardrock miner, age 34, made $1 per day while trapping game. A carpenter, age 63, had a "well-built cabin" on his own mining claim and rotated between the gold field in summer and Pasadena, California, in winter, where he practiced his other trade.

A couple, ages not given, lived in a trailer on the Yuba River near a town named Timbuctoo, a prosperous camp in the 1850s and 1860s. Jointly, they made $3 per day and $500 per season. They had built their own trailer from the profit of one good day of $22. The husband had been a pipefitter with an oil company until 1930. They had rotated in the fruit region from 1930 to 1934. Another former pipefitter, age 51, and his wife also lived on the Yuba River in a tent. They averaged $2 per day or $400 per year. They had no regular work since 1933. A couple, ages not given, lived in a large house as caretakers so they paid no rent. They made extra from taking in tourists as well as placering part-time without royalty. A husband, age 59, and wife, age 30, made $2 per day for about 100 days per year and operated a roadside stand which made $100 more per year.

Two families, one in a tent, the other in an adjacent trailer, had worked together in oil fields in southern California. They used a three h.p. gasoline engine to recover $100 each over a 3½ month season. These families also had small incomes from rental property in southern California. A family of six lived in town. Two older children were in school; two younger ones placered with the parents. This family also rotated to fruit farms in season. A couple lived in a tent on the American River and the husband had a full-time job but the wife mined and recovered $.25 per day. Another couple alternated between logging camps, where the young husband drove a

Caterpillar tractor, and placer mines, where they lived in a tent. He made $600 per year, $100 of that from placers.[45]

Finally, full-time miners reported these interesting circumstances. A farmer, age 57, on the Klamath River in northwest California supplemented his income with $300 per year placering. A pensioner, aged 70, drew $15 per month from his fund and $.10 per day placering on the Stanislaus River. Another pensioner had lost an arm and leg but was still able to make $125 per year working placers to supplement his $8 monthly check. A 72-year-old man owned his own claim and cabin as well as ranch land. An elderly miner, age 85, on the Illinois River in Oregon also supported his retarded son. Family unity stands out in many aspects of life in the 1930s.

A former baker, aged 64, worked 250 days per year, averaging six hours per day. He paid some royalty, but still netted $120.00 per year. A former hardrock miner, age 74, drew $30.00 monthly as a Spanish-American War veteran, and $.35 per day placering. Two partners, ages 41 and 60, came to California in 1933 after reading newspaper stories on placer mining. The older man drew a small pension and made $.30 per day gold mining.

A miner, age 60, used a three-quarter h.p. gasoline engine to make $.50 per day. A former carpenter, age 47, found a four h.p. engine could deliver $.75 per day in his area. A woman, age 40, worked a creek in the Sierra Nevada Mountains above the more frequented Mother Lode. She also prospected and had been a real estate agent. A one-armed man aged 64 drew a pension of $10.00 per month and earned $.50 per day placering and prospecting.

Another prospector who made $.50 to $.60 per day placer mining lived in Mariposa County, California. He had come from New York where he had been an auto mechanic but had to sell his tools along the way to make the trip and was unable to return to his trade. Also placer mining in Mariposa County were a vineyardist who had lost his vineyard and an unemployed water well driller.

Mariposa County had one family of particular interest. A former sawmill worker and his wife and two young children had been placer mining on a royalty basis but it applied only if they exceeded a certain level. They made $400 per year but were still below the unspecified level. Every day the father was seen rowing the children to the school bus stop across the river where they waited in a shelter that he had built.

An operator at Gold Hill, Jackson County, Oregon, was perhaps the most prosperous of any in the survey. He had been at the same location since 1926 and estimated his total take over the years at $2,800. He paid a 20 percent royalty to the owners of the private land.

Two partners, ages 48 and 55, paid a royalty of 15 percent and still made $400 in 1937. They had dug a long ditch for water supply. A miner, age 48, lived in a truck fitted for placer development. He reported making $1,200 the previous year in Nevada. A miner, age 40, on the Yuba River in California made $2 per day for 200 days using a sluice box and a small wing dam. Two miners only described as "young" used a pump on their own claim to make $500 per year.

An owner of placer lands worked them himself in northwest California while two others also worked there; the report is unclear as to their status. The first was a 34-year-old widower with three children who had last been farming in the state of Washington. The second was a former sea diver, age 49. No other details were given but the present writer has long noticed that individuals with interests in mining, underwater exploration, and maps of lost treasure are looking for the same thing—gold—and these groups often overlap. As an example, an article in the *Prescott Evening Courier* on July 14, 1931, related how Adolph Ruth had dropped a long-standing career with the federal government in Washington to come to the West to mine. However, he had gotten caught up in a search for the Lost Dutchman mine in the Superstition Mountains near Phoenix, Arizona, and had disappeared. His son had begun a search for him.

Three miners, ages not stated, on the Trinity River in California each made $2 per day. They paid rental on the claim and cabin. These miners were the only ones mentioned in the report who used hydraulic methods (discussed in more detail in chapter 6). They had access to a stream at higher elevation than the gold-bearing banks so they could successfully use this process.

Two miners who lived in a tent made $800. One was a dairy farmer who had lost his dairy. The second stated that he had attended the Colorado School of Mines for three years and was a World War I veteran. A particularly "ingenious" miner used an auto differential to build his own small dredge, which yielded $3 per day over 150 days. Equally ingenious was an unemployed blacksmith and welder, age 44, who used a pump on a wheelbarrow to make $3 per day for a total of $500 per year.

A miner age 54 stated that he had graduated from a major eastern university where he had been an All-American fullback. Subsequently he had been a building contractor in southern California and had made as much as $10,000 per year. He reported placer earnings at $1.45 per day. Another party who had owned his own mining claim since 1932 had made $5.00 per day for an annual total of $500.00 to $600.00. He had a particularly nice home with a modern range and other appliances.

A former quartz (hardrock) miner, age 40, made $3.00 per day for a total of $400.00 in a year, despite the fact that he was suffering from silicosis. He lived in a tent and had an old automobile. A World War I veteran, age 55, and his wife both mined for $2.00 to $3.00 per week and had a 16-year-old daughter who did no mining. They had received relief since a pension had ended in 1933. Another World War I veteran, age 51, had a family of five including boys 16 and 18 who helped in gold recovery. They received a pension of $30.00 per month and $.25 per day working placers.

A 69-year-old miner who had trekked to one of the truly classic gold rushes of all time—Alaska in 1898—received a pension of $30.00 per month plus small returns from working placers. His wife made beaded articles for sale to tourists. Another elderly couple from the state of Washington found themselves "gold mining by accident." They made $.15 to $.25 per day while their only son, who was in the CCC, sent $25.00 per month. Still another elderly couple on the Salmon River in Idaho made $.20 per day. The husband, age 59, had been a medical doctor in Kansas but had been crippled.

Another miner working near Randsburg 45 miles northeast of Mojave in southern California also had an interesting personal background. This man, age 64, and his wife, 55, had been drywashing in the desert region since 1932. He had been doorkeeper at the U.S. Senate when his uncle was a senator from North Dakota.

A disabled World War I veteran drew a pension of $100.00 per month and made $.75 per day from placers. He and his wife and seven children had tried several places. This individual also had an interesting personal background having received considerable training as an aviation mechanic and pilot.

On the Trinity River another World War I veteran, age 48, and his

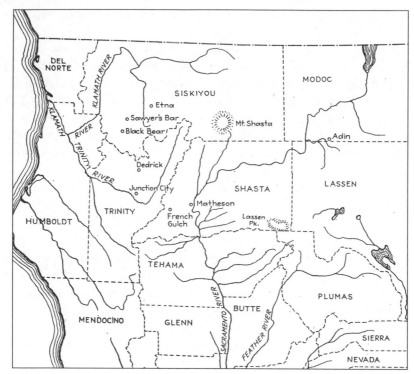

*Map 2—California's far northwestern gold region where both hydraulic
mining and dredging were profitable.* Engineering and Mining Journal *135,
no. 11, p. 516 (used by permission of Maclean Hunter Publishing Co.).*

wife had remodeled an old cabin into a comfortable home. He had
been an auto mechanic until his health failed. An unemployed truck
driver, age 53, and his wife used an auto engine to move boulders to
get buried gravel. A former farmer, age 58, with his wife and four-
year-old daughter, had much larger equipment than most could afford, including a 60 h.p. engine and scraper, which helped him
recover $2.00 to $2.50 per day since February of 1933.

A former teacher, age 50, had made $2,000 per year at a private
trade school in Los Angeles but that ended in 1930. He and his wife
made $450 per year on the Yuba River; their two children lived with
relatives. A widower, aged 36, supported four children in a tent by
working seven day weeks for nearly the full year. He had been a radio technician but preferred placering because of his asthma.[46]

The preliminary report of 1937 had very little data on the lives of individuals. Two brief notes from Colorado do merit recording. A New York City druggist with his own store had come to Colorado for one month to "investigate placering." Two Detroit youths "cussed the propaganda of the unprospected empire of Gunnison County" as put forth in promotional literature, but they kept on trying. The research team estimated that placer miners in Colorado worked an average of 60 days per year and annually recovered $146.[47]

The Bureau of Mines/WPA research team was critical of what they saw as only positive reports of mining successes and the impetus this had given to the automobile gold rush participants. In contrast to that view are the many negative stories the present writer has cited throughout the present volume. In juxtaposition to these supposedly positive stories were others that plainly stated the truth—that the great majority of participants were not finding fortunes. The best examples of the latter are the *Saturday Evening Post* articles cited in the previous chapter. Authorities such as Walter Bradley and other representatives of official agencies issued reports that stimulated interest, but they too maintained a realistic view about success, as did many guidebooks and instructors teaching courses in gold recovery.

The Bureau of Mines/WPA study generally focused on those who were unable to sell directly to the U.S. Mint and failed to include small business firms which did sell to the mint but which were still essentially amateur operations. Such firms certainly were important and merit discussion. One modest placer operation in Gilpin County, Colorado, provides an unusual amount of data on this aspect of mining which was derived from a study done by the *Engineering and Mining Journal* that made extensive observations of procedures and profit margins in 1934.

This firm, the Pommel Mining Co. of Denver, operated for only about 200 days per year because of snow pack at high elevation. (The Mother Lode generally had a season from May to October, depending on rains. Northwest California and Oregon had a season in the spring and early summer.) Pommel employed ten regular workers at $3 per day plus three shovel operators who drew $1 per hour. These skilled workers ran a dragline, a heavy piece of earthmoving equipment. The dragline used a bucket to deliver 50 cubic yards per hour into a device called a "dredge" which was actually by description a floating washing plant. The firm had two salaried employees, a general manager who made $250 per month, and a superintendent who made $200 per month, and paid a royalty to the owners of 76 acres of mining claims.

To make the most of the short season, the operation worked on three shifts and functioned 24 hours a day. Other costs included fuel for two Ford industrial engines, depreciation on machinery, State Workmen's Compensation (the only government mandate then), and maintenance, which included a shutdown of 5½ days per month. The operation processed gravel for $.139 per cubic yard, though realistically gold content needed to average $.20 per cubic yard or more to make a profit. Of course values could vary considerably within a particular area.[48]

As early as the end of the 1933 placering season, the *Engineering and Mining Journal* reported that 25 percent of total U.S. gold production was from placers. Of this, some 64 dredges provided 70 percent. Clearly suitable machinery could do far better than poorly equipped individuals. It is obvious that heavy equipment multiplied returns.[49]

Though overall placer production was up massively by 1939, the smaller operators had been dwindling in the preceding several years. The 3 percent that the Census did not even count but that the Bureau of Mines surveyed apparently constituted a large number of individuals who were developed enough to call themselves small businesses. In Colorado, the Bureau of Mines found 967 small businesses in 1934, 842 in 1935, and 700 in 1936. Ironically, the *Engineering and Mining Journal* saw this decline as "a sign of better times" when it reported the figures in 1937. The journal stated that "expanding operations in mining districts are believed to have attracted these small operators to jobs in the mines or mills." Whether this was true, or just editorial speculation, is impossible to determine. Small operators were depleting those areas available to them and could not immediately learn technical underground mining. Also, New Deal work programs may have absorbed many of them.[50]

Returning to questions asked earlier in this study: was the return to gold mining in the 1930s a manifestation primarily of the frontier school interpretation of western history, or was it a manifestation instead of the modern industrial age and the evolving vast, interlocking world-wide economy?

Placer mining was clearly related to social ills and evolved in response to suffering in the Depression. Families and individuals who participated in the automobile gold rush were self-selected from the general population because they shared a frontier psychological perspective or were willing to develop such a viewpoint. As stated in the Introduction, "The frontier thesis includes a psychological outlook that the West can provide some form of solution to any problem that may emerge. Such an outlook extends to large scale national problems as well as individual problems." Certainly, this was the driving factor sending thousands of people to recreate some of the classic events of the past century—the placer gold rushes. Elements of the original events clearly recurred: egalitarianism, self-reliance, optimism, and a search for economic prosperity. As might be expected, newspapers in the immediate areas of activity stressed the frontier connection, but reporters for several national publications based in places like New York and Philadelphia also suggested this spirit. The authors of a lengthy, official government report fall into a similar category. Egalitarianism was particularly evident in the participation of women and members of racial and ethnic minorities. Optimism is more subjective and more difficult to measure; however, enough observers noticed it in contrast to the general outlook of the early 1930s to definitely cite this as another major factor.

However, by the 1930s industrial and economic development in the West had made that region an integral a part of an evolving world-wide economy and as such had brought in major sources of capital for development of resources at an industrial level. The questions, then, are not mutually exclusive and there are two correct answers.

Politics

A brief overview of political events in the late 1800s and early 1900s provides a foundation for understanding gold policies in the 1930s. During the latter part of the nineteenth century, gold and silver became significant issues in partisan national politics. In 1873 Congress quietly passed the Coinage Act, which ended purchases of silver by the Treasury Department and allowed the U.S. Mint to produce only token amounts of new silver coins. Soon after its passage, farm crop prices collapsed, and farming groups and their political representatives blamed the Coinage Act calling it the "Crime of '73." Debtor farmers in the South and the Great Plains demanded that Congress enact "free and unlimited coinage of silver," which would require the U.S. Mint to buy all silver brought to it and place it into circulation mostly as silver dollars. The new silver in circulation would inflate the currency enough to improve crop prices and would allow farmers to repay debts with money possessing less buying power.[1]

The parties involved in silver mining, both management and labor alike, naturally favored free silver, and the political leadership of the movement could count on the support of several silver-producing western states. Opponents were usually associated with banking and commercial interests in the East, but any creditor who stood to lose from inflation was likely to oppose free silver. The opponents acquired the unearned title "sound money men."

In 1878 the silver interests secured passage of the Bland-Allison Act, which required the Treasury to buy and coin at least $2 million worth of silver a month, but the measure fell far short of producing noticeable inflation. In the 1880s economic prosperity returned without the impetus of free silver and the issue lost much of its earlier momentum.

Resistance to free silver had centered on its relative value compared to gold, which for much of U.S. history had been 16 ounces of silver to 1 ounce of gold, or a figure fairly close to that ratio, with the U.S. Mint making periodic adjustments in the content of coins as the real ratio changed. By the 1890s, the ratio of 16 to 1 provided a marked subsidy to silver producers since the fixed price of gold was $20.67; the net result was that the federal government was buying silver at $1.29 per ounce, over twice the market price in 1894. Historically, federal policy had allowed ready exchange of silver at the Treasury for gold. Since the value of silver coins was less than their face value and they could be exchanged for gold at face value, people exchanged their silver dollars for gold dollars draining gold from the Treasury.

Despite severe demands on the government's gold reserves, during his first term in 1884, President Grover Cleveland steadfastly adhered to the gold standard and requested that Congress repeal the Bland-Allison Act, but Congress refused.

The election of Benjamin Harrison in 1888 displaced Cleveland and witnessed the reversal of many of his policies. Harrison's administration increased silver purchases, and in 1890 a glut on the silver market led to Congressional passage of the Sherman Silver Purchase Act, a measure intended primarily to aid the mining industry and stipulating the Treasury purchase 4.5 million ounces of silver per month or approximately twice the amount authorized by the Bland-Allison Act.

At the end of Harrison's term, Americans were ready for a return to Cleveland's policies, but a severe financial panic occurred shortly after he was elected for a second term in 1893. Cleveland felt the panic, which caused 15,000 business failures and led to 4 million people being out of work, was the result of the Sherman Silver Purchase Act. Congress repealed the silver purchase clause in the act in June 1893 at a special session called by President Cleveland.

Cleveland became a leader among "sound money men" even though he was a Democrat, but his position on the gold standard led many in his own party to view him as no different than the opposition, and perhaps worse. It was obvious that silver forces would capture the Democratic Convention of 1896, but there was great uncertainty as to who their presidential candidate would be. With Cleveland out of contention, a former Populist,[2] 36-year-old William

Jennings Bryan of Nebraska, used free silver to gain the Democratic Party's presidential nomination. In one of the most famous speeches in American history, he swung the convention to nominate him with the immortal line, "You shall not press down upon the brow of labor this crown of thorns, you shall not crucify mankind on a cross of gold!"[3]

Bryan waged an energetic campaign, but even though he swept the mining states, the South, and some agricultural prairie states, as expected, he lost the Northeast and Midwest and the farming states of North Dakota, Minnesota, and Iowa.[4] Republican William McKinley became the twenty-fifth president of the United States instead.

The free silver supporters had viewed the West as the key to improving the entire economy but they had failed to realize that major gold deposits remained to be discovered. California was still producing some placer gold, and lode gold came from Idaho, Colorado, and Arizona, but the majority of great discoveries of the 1870s and 1880s had been in silver. There had been new gold discoveries in the Black Hills of South Dakota at the Homestake Mine in 1876, but production was not sufficient to affect the overall monetary situation.

When major new gold discoveries did come into full production, they not only provided jobs for the miners but provided sufficient new gold to inflate the currency without free silver. The most important mining district in the 1890s proved to be Cripple Creek, Colorado, though many authors have not even mentioned this remarkable area as having an effect on the nation's recovery from the panic and depression of 1893. Gold, with its fixed price of $20.67, naturally attracted the attention of investors, especially since almost all other prices were falling abruptly.

The introduction of new gold into the economy strengthened an economic recovery that had begun just prior to McKinley's election, and Cripple Creek began to show its potential with roasting of the telluride ores followed by cyanide extraction, which allowed more recovery. The cyanide process also aided in extracting other previously unworkable gold-bearing ores, many of which were in tailings of older mines. Then, in 1898 the Klondike rush to Canada's Yukon resulted in the bulk of the recovered gold being sent to the United States. The Klondike stimulated discoveries in neighboring Alaska;

in Australia and South Africa other major gold strikes and cyanide processing resulted in sufficient gold to boost supplies on a world-wide basis. A final discovery in yet another "overlooked" locale, Tonopah and Goldfield, Nevada, in 1902, helped preserve prosperity until World War I.[5]

With an improved economy in the early twentieth century, free silver became an issue that seemed no more than a historical footnote. World War I and the 1920s continued general good times, despite a brief downturn in 1921, but 1929 brought back painful memories of 1873 and 1893, and a return to the economic idea of free silver that had been seen as way to end earlier economic depressions.

By 1931, a grass-roots movement had organized at Denver to obtain passage of an act providing for "free and unlimited coinage of gold and silver and in their use as money at a natural and rational ratio." By the next year the movement called a convention, which met in the legislative chambers of the Colorado State Capitol Building, and the featured speaker was none other than William Jennings Bryan, Jr. The younger Bryan, a practicing attorney in Arizona, recognized the importance of gold but stressed that the two metals, gold and silver, "should supplement each other." Free silver was taking on new political life, and several western senators had been quietly working on revival of the idea for a number of years. Eventually it would go before the U.S. Congress.[6]

Soon the new version of the free silver movement had spread throughout the western United States. School children memorized Bryan's "Cross of Gold" speech along with the Preamble to the Constitution and the Gettysburg Address. Mining communities followed events closely. A nationally reported story accurately reflected the situation: "The sick metal, silver, has refused to take heart at the latest curative measures."[7]

Ironically, President Herbert Hoover, a mining engineer by profession, had resisted all attempts to resurrect free silver policies, any of which would have aided the mining industry, but was enamored with the traditional gold standard. He saw Cleveland's and McKinley's adherence to it as being crucial to long-term economic stability. Hoover endorsed the 1932 Glass-Steagall Act, which made $750 million in government gold available for industrial and business purposes, thus preventing a further downward slide in the economy. Well-known Hoover biographer Joan Hoff Wilson has cited this action plus the development of the Reconstruction Finance Corporation (R.F.C.) as crucial in preventing a complete economic collapse in 1932. Hoover believed that the Federal Reserve Board was largely responsible for the Depression and that it was pursuing policies that were counterproductive; the release of gold served to balance the malpractice of the Federal Reserve.

Joan Hoff Wilson and other authorities have stated that the New Deal simply copied Glass-Steagall and the R.F.C. In fact, Roosevelt's actions were larger in scale and more long-term. The United States had first adopted the gold standard in 1879 because Great Britain had adopted it, and Hoover continued to maintain the gold standard, even though Great Britain terminated adherence to that policy in 1931.[8]

Silver emerged as a significant issue at the national convention of the Democratic Party in 1932, and, as in the last century, also arose among a small but determined group of westerners at the Republican convention as well. However, one leading Republican, William E. Borah of Idaho, did not even attend. Borah knew that silver was a hopeless cause in his own party, and he boycotted the convention and failed to endorse nominee Herbert Hoover. John H. Hammond, a prominent, wealthy Republican and a mining engineer by trade, joined Borah in supporting free silver. However, the *Idaho Daily Statesman*, which generally supported Borah, was one of the few newspapers in the West to oppose aid to silver.[9]

It appeared that the resurrection of the silver issue might even result in a "silver plank" being written into the platform at the Democratic convention in the summer of 1932, but ultimately a voice vote from the convention floor denied the measure. As in any Presidential contest, the ideas and opinions of the nominee count for far more than the party platform anyway, and in 1932 the nominee was none other than Franklin D. Roosevelt. Mr. Roosevelt's appearance and style of public speaking proved to be major assets offsetting the fact that he shied away from discussing many issues in detail. However, one specific speech does stand out as a statement of policy. Before a huge, enthusiastic crowd in Butte, Montana, on September 20, 1932, FDR picked up the spirit of Bryan by stating "silver must be restored as a monetary metal, and the Democratic pledge on the subject must be kept."[10] There was no denying the impact and focus of that statement, which was accentuated by the site where it was spoken.

Roosevelt won by a landslide. He issued Executive Orders which abandoned the gold standard for domestic matters on April 5, 1933, and for foreign matters on April 20. Certain terms of these orders were controversial. It became illegal to own any significant amounts of gold and individuals and commercial banks were required to surrender virtually all gold to the Federal Reserve Banks. The only exceptions were rare coins, "reasonable" amounts for use in industry and the arts, and a maximum of $100 per person in gold coin and certificates, which had been a major portion of the circulating currency. The government redeemed coin and certificates at face value and other gold at $20.67 per ounce, the standard price. Despite the orders, large holdings of gold coin and even bullion remained in private hands. Today many gold coins are available to collectors which were not defined as "rare" in 1933 because their owners had quietly retained them. However, the holders of most paper gold certificates did cash them in.[11]

The president had already begun purchases of large amounts of gold even though he withdrew all paper certificates exchangeable for it. Congress saw the need for a new definition of the Uniform Value of Coins and Currencies as part of the end of the gold standard, and debates on the issues were complex and heated.[12] Representative Martin F. Smith, Democrat from Washington, stated, "The enactment of this law is another emancipation proclamation, declaring liberty for 120 million Americans from the thralldom and cruel yoke of gold which has enslaved the human race."[13] Emotions ran high, as the transcripts of the debate reveal, but the bill, which became an Act to Establish the Uniform Value of Coins and Currencies, passed the House on May 29, 1933, by 283 to 57 with 1 present but not voting and 90 not attending. The Senate rehashed the House arguments, then voted 48–20 for the bill, with 28 not voting, on June 3.[14] This action demonstrates the strength of the new Democratic majority in Congress, which accomplished so much during the "Hundred Days" of the New Deal.

The principles of the act were retained in the subsequent more considered Gold Reserve Act of 1934. Though both houses debated this bill at length, the final tally of 360 to 40 (with 32 not voting) by which the House approved and the Senate count of 66 to 23 (7 not voting) showed the strong sentiments in its favor. Representative Martin Dies of Texas was not alone when he expressed regret that the law did not go farther.[15]

The Gold Reserve Act of 1934 allowed the president to fix the weight of the gold dollar at a lower figure. On January 31, one day after signing the bill, Roosevelt designated the weight to be 15 and 5/21 grains, a reduction of 41 percent. Roosevelt had been ordering higher prices of gold purchases by the government on a day-to-day basis since October 1933 but had not set a permanent price or revalued the dollar. Now the official price of gold rose to $35 an ounce, where it stayed until the early 1970s. The primary reason for the adjustment was to allow the same amount of gold to back a larger proportion of paper currency and to increase the holdings in dollars for foreign trade. Domestic prices were affected only marginally, but the action caused imports to become more expensive in U.S. dollars, while giving foreign buyers an advantage in purchasing U.S. goods. The degree of domestic inflation, however, failed to attain what had been anticipated.

One commentator on the situation was the inimitable humorist Will Rogers, who was certainly the most widely read commentator of the Depression era. His column appeared on the front pages of almost all American newspapers. Rogers always made his common-sense remarks in a down-home style, complete with his unique spelling and grammatical constructions reflecting his origins among the common man. By 1934, he too approved going off the gold standard, with some reservations.

> But on the other hand lowering the price of money from a dollar to 59 cents dident have quite the effect that the economists thought it would. They had figured that it would raise prices 40 cents on the dollar, well it was just one of those theories that worked fine with a pencil, but dident work with money. . . . You can take 40 cents off the American Dollar in terms of foreign money. But the old boy here at home thats not going to Europe still thinks it's a dollar.[16]

The price change caused gold production to skyrocket until World War II. The estimated 1933 U.S. mine production level had remained in the same range as the preceding decade—at 2,292,000 ounces; the 1934 estimated figure reached 2,779,000 ounces, but this increase of 21 percent proved to be only a warm up. By 1937 the estimated total reached 4,117,000 ounces, and in 1941 it peaked at 4,751,000 ounces, a yearly volume of gold that had never occurred before and probably has not occurred since (although production in the late 1970s and early 1980s was high). Some of the later figures were derived from masses of gold coming from Europe, but purchases from U.S. mines still accounted for a large part of the dramatic rise.[17]

The congressional acts relating to gold during the Depression carried much of the sentiment of Bryan and Populism, but a true fulfillment of that sentiment had to involve silver. Leading the silver faction were Senators Burton Wheeler of Montana, Key Pittman of Nevada, and Elmer Thomas of Oklahoma, though senators and representatives of both parties from all the western states were active in the move. For example, Idaho's William E. Borah and James P. Pope, a Republican and a New Deal Democrat respectively, emphatically agreed on the silver issue.

In examining events during the New Deal era related to the silver issue, a number of well-known historians, including Arthur M. Schlesinger, Jr., and William Leuchtenburg, have focused on the Silver Purchase Act FDR ultimately signed on June 19, 1934. However, the Silver Act was just the finale to what had been a movement by the pro-silver congressional delegation.

On May 12, 1933, silver faction leader Senator Elmer Thomas of Oklahoma added an amendment to a farm relief bill that allowed the president to adjust the weight of silver at a definite fixed ratio to the gold dollar. This meant that the President could set a higher price for silver purchased by the government. Also the Treasury could accept silver at a rate of up to $.50 per ounce from foreign governments in payment of their debts to the United States. The most important provisions theoretically provided for the fulfillment of Bryan's original dream—the president could order unlimited coinage of both gold and silver at a fixed ratio.

The silver faction had Roosevelt's broad statement at Butte, Montana, during the campaign, to give them confidence that he would follow through, even though there is some evidence that Roosevelt was merely giving "lip service" to the silver faction to draw their sup-

Fig. 12—*Key Pittman, U.S. Senator from Nevada, had long sought passage of a silver purchase act by Congress. Courtesy U.S. Senate Historical Office, Washington, D.C.*

port for other New Deal policies. He proved remarkably reluctant in fulfilling his promise, even though it was one of the most specific statements he offered during the campaign.

On December 21, 1933, Roosevelt ordered a price of 64.64 cents per ounce for silver to be paid by the mint for the next four years. At the time the market price was $.44. Roosevelt's price was one-half of the ratio of 16 ounces of silver to 1 ounce of gold, or $1.29 per

Fig. 13—Burton K. Wheeler, U.S. Senator from Montana, had a long record as a progressive when he advocated silver purchases. Courtesy U.S. Senate Historical Office, Washington, D.C.

ounce. He designated the figure of $1.29 per ounce as the value of the silver for currency backing. The government was buying silver at a subsidized price well above the market price but then designating currency backed with it at twice that value.[18] The price increase was certainly enough to begin to stimulate the industry, and stocks of silver mining companies jumped as much as 50 percent at the opening of the New York Stock Exchange the day after the announcement. But the limitation of only four years made the situation less favorable for the long term. Also, the Treasury printed additional silver certificates, adding modestly to the overall money supply and promoting slight inflation.

The silver faction skillfully consolidated its support in the Second Session, and Senator Burton Wheeler of Montana and Senator William H. King of Utah proposed a silver purchase clause in the Gold Reserve Act of 1934.[19] The administration was split over monetary policy at this time. Gold purchases had caused dissention in the ranks of Roosevelt's advisors, and the president himself realized that the silver faction was growing and took an open position opposing it. He sent top advisor Dr. Raymond Moley to attempt to talk Wheeler out of the proposal, but to no avail.[20]

The silver faction then tried attaching a silver amendment to another farm bill, the same ploy that had worked the previous year when Senator Thomas' amendment to the farm relief bill had passed, but they were forced to remove it when Roosevelt threatened a veto. Undeterred, westerners in the House offered it again under the informal title of the Pittman bill. It required government purchases of silver until the Treasury's supply of the metal reached one-fourth the total market value of the gold stock or until the market price reached $1.29 per ounce in an effort to place more silver certificates in circulation. It also provided for a more permanent, long-term requirement for silver purchases.[21]

The House considered and approved the Pittman bill (designated H.R. 9745) by an overwhelming 272–37 on June 6, 1934; obviously the issue was bipartisan and had a level of emotional appeal that went far beyond the mining states.[22] In the Senate, Elmer Thomas of Oklahoma proposed a realistic amendment to remonetize the currency with new certificates redeemable in silver or gold, thus establishing true bimetallism. Thomas noted that without his amendment the proposed bill could cause silver to rise to $1.29 per ounce (the old 16 to 1 ratio), which would prove costly to the government.[23]

As the Pittman bill had moved through Congress, it attracted the attention of those European nations that still viewed gold as a detriment to their own trade potentials. The leader of the Bank of France said that it was "just another economic experiment before the U.S. returns to a gold standard"—an assessment that was obviously in error in the long-run in the history not only of the United States but the industrial world.[24]

Senator Thomas' amendment to the Pittman bill failed. Subsequent similar amendments by flamboyant firebrand Senator Huey P. Long of Louisiana to the Pittman bill failed, even though Long made a speech on June 9 portraying Bryan as a "true Democrat" and castigating the long dead Grover Cleveland as a traitor for having been a "gold Democrat," hence really a Republican. The Senate voted 55 to 25 (16 not voting) in favor.[25]

As part of the policies regarding both gold and silver, Congress ordered construction of major new depositories to securely store both metals. The gold depository at Ft. Knox, Kentucky, became one of the most famous federal facilities outside Washington, D.C., and the initial cost of the granite structure ran to $560,000. The first gold bullion arrived in early 1937. Though the silver depository was just as well constructed, it did not gain the fame of its sister facility, but then silver has always been the runner-up to gold. The silver depository, built at West Point, New York, had a capacity of $2 billion at 1930s prices.[26]

The Silver Purchase Act, which FDR signed on June 19, 1934, essentially finalized what the silver-producing states had wanted. It was also enough to convince the president to follow through with the authority he in fact already possessed—to subsidize the industry over an extended period by issuing massive amounts of new currency (either in coins, silver certificates, or even unbacked notes). However, he still only modestly increased the money supply, and his reluctance to follow through led some free silver supporters to keep up the movement even after FDR signed the Silver Purchase Act. Always the master politician, he had endorsed the bill with a major statement on May 22, but it was a *fait accompli* by that time.[27]

Will Rogers addressed the Silver Act in his characteristic style when it passed Congress with one of his most famous opening lines.

> Well all I know is just what I read in the papers. Well air you know Dillinger dropped out there for awhile and the papers just dropped off to almost nothing. Then, too, Congress was behaving itself for a short period, and that hurt the news. (Course it helped the country.). . .
>
> I am just like a lot of others, I don't know just what silver being made a money will do to us. It seems like it ought to help. But thats what we pay those birds in Washington ten thousand a year for, is to argue over such nonsettleable things.[28]

Fig. 14 — The gold depository at Ft. Knox, Kentucky, became one of the most famous federal facilities outside Washington, D.C. The initial cost of the granite structure ran to $560,000. The first gold bullion arrived in early 1937. Courtesy National Archives, Washington, D.C.

The legislators from the mining states had already achieved the best economic situation for their particular constituencies. With silver purchases added to gold, the mining economies were the most prosperous in the nation, while the Depression made other commodity prices low. Inflation, the second aspect of the free silver movement, would actually prove a marked disadvantage for the mining states, though the more populous agricultural regions would presumably benefit.

Even with their own region benefitting, Congress members from the mining states kept up the fight for inflation, to their credit. Two days after the law took effect, senators Borah of Idaho and Wheeler of Montana condemned the administration follow-up of the law as inadequate. Senators Thomas of Oklahoma and Long of Louisiana joined in this assessment, but their constituencies were obviously on the receiving end of inflation benefits. The four senators made these charges despite the fact that Secretary of the Treasury Morgenthau was trying to portray the administration policy as favorably as possible, while leaving out any specific reference to exact purchase volume. Still, the fact that the strong majorities for silver purchases did not continue for silver-backed inflation is rather surprising. The issue was still simmering as late as 1939.[29]

By October 1934, Colorado's new senator, Edward P. Costigan, reported that gold and silver production was "comparable to the boom days of a quarter century ago," but he believed that there was even greater potential available from the higher prices.[30]

Several other major political issues of the 1930s also affected mining and were reflections of the Depression, though none of these were as significant as prices paid for gold and silver. The most long-lasting revolved around annual assessments for mining claims that had not gone to full private ownership, known as patent.

Under the Mining Law of 1872, private parties could stake mining claims on many federal lands and remove any mineral deposits, if they could be worked profitably. The mining law stated that the claimant had to perform $100 worth of improvements per year to legally maintain each claim prior to full ownership purchase process. This $100 in improvements is usually called "annual assessment work."

The Depression provided grounds for claimants to petition Congress for exemptions from the annual assessment requirement. Presumably many claim holders were otherwise occupied and simply could not perform the annual assessment work, so Congress passed exemptions for each year beginning in 1932, but did so in separate acts year by year. The suspension of the annual assessment requirement affected the entire West throughout the Depression, and the suspension was also valid in Alaska, except in 1936 and 1937. Miners did have to file a simple notice with the local recorder, usually at the county courthouse, that they intended to hold the claims. Forms were available at any newspaper office or general store in mining areas.

Yet the very passage of the suspension of actual performance of annual assessment work was ironic because hardrock mining, with its subsidies at guaranteed mint prices for both gold and silver, had generally been the least depressed element in the national economy following the low metal prices of 1931–33. Even the *Engineering and Mining Journal* editorialized against suspending annual assessment since failure of a claim holder to perform the work would simply abandon the claim to others who would be more interested in actual development. However, Congress continued to exempt annual assessments even in World War II and well after.[31]

Obviously Congress wanted to encourage mining as much as possible and did so by making the traditional Mining Law of 1872 less stringent for the small miner and prospector, the "little man" who the law had been designed to aid. President Roosevelt apparently agreed since he signed an act in June of 1934 which specifically and expressly continued the mining law despite other long-term changes in public land policy. However, by 1937 Secretary of the Interior Harold Ickes was calling for an end to mining claims and advocated instead a leasing system similar to that instituted for oil and gas in 1920. At the time Ickes stood virtually alone, and no serious movement to repeal the Mining Law of 1872 would emerge until the 1960s. Despite some recent modifications, the basic claims system still survives in 1998.[32]

Other New Deal legislation affected mining. One of the most controversial of the agencies was the National Recovery Administration (N.R.A.), which is best remembered for the "blue eagle" emblem that it widely displayed. The N.R.A. required various groupings of businesses to write codes for that particular industry's wages, working conditions, prices, and production. The fact that industries wrote their own codes provided the most controversy. In fact, the N.R.A. only lasted two years when a unanimous U.S. Supreme Court decision ruled it unconstitutional. In the interim it had become an administrative nightmare. Further, the chief administrator, retired General Hugh Johnson, proved a severe embarrassment when media attention on the agency also revealed his alcoholism. Many New Dealers confidentially stated that they were pleased to see it end.[33]

The mining industry generally spoke up favorably for the N.R.A. More than most industries, mining had a clear-cut set of products and prices and easily defined jobs. However, there were some critics in the industry, as with the nation. The Placerville (California) *Mountain Democrat* of April 13, 1934, summed up the situation and the gold possession issue in a succinct sentence: "We're patriotic, but we'd prefer gold eagles to blue ones" (gold coins that were worth $10 were nicknamed eagles; the blue eagle was the symbol of the N.R.A.). As early as September of 1933, the *Engineering and Mining Journal* had credited the N.R.A. with improving mining by initiating copper and lead/zinc codes. By March 1935, just a few months before the N.R.A. ended, Louis Cates, president of copper giant Phelps Dodge Corporation, stated, "The code has worked satisfactorily. It has provided for the collection of reliable information that has led to a more intelligent conduct of business and the industry." However, following the Supreme Court decision, the editor of the *Engineering and Mining Journal* dismissed the N.R.A. abruptly, noting that the new federal committee was writing an overall National Mineral Resource Policy that would be far more important.[34]

As important employers, the mining industries also became subject to provisions of the N.R.A. regarding labor organization. The Wagner Act of 1935 included further provisions in this area. The new National Labor Relations Board administered special elections to organize labor unions in individual plants and to mediate disputes. Union organizers in the East used the Wagner Act to organize many coal miners there; however, the generally prosperous state of western mining led to relatively little labor activism. It is true that the work forces in a number of mines voted to recognize unions, most frequently the International Union of Mine, Mill, and Smelter Workers, but most miners were content to accept the wages offered, which were generally quite good in gold and silver mines.[35]

The New Deal also promoted health and safety legislation in a number of areas. Miners had long suffered from silicosis or miners' consumption. Safety and health issues first attracted political attention in the early twentieth century. Newer mining drills used water to suppress the dust that caused silicosis after miners breathed it over the years. The New Deal went so far as to adopt the slogan "Stop the Dust," and new safety requirements generated an important secondary market for mining related equipment.[36]

Russell F. Flarty recalled the new safety consciousness of the later 1930s in an interview with the author on September 14, 1996. Flarty was a skilled underground miner from Boulder County, Colorado. When he began his career in 1936, he used an antique power drill, which lacked a separate water line to lubricate the bit and to suppress the dust. About a year later the campaign to "Stop the Dust" had forced his employer to replace the old drills. Flarty emphasized that this was the most significant technical change that he personally experienced in over three decades of skilled underground mining in approximately ten different mines. He firmly be-

Fig. 15—*The silver subsidy provided an additional incentive for mining firms to purchase the latest machinery, like this Allis-Chalmers hoist from major manufacturers of industrial equipment.* Engineering and Mining Journal *139, no. 3, p. 75 (used by permission of Maclean Hunter Publishing Co.).*

lieved that it probably saved him from silicosis in later life. Indeed, the only other technical improvement that Flarty noted was the replacement of carbide lamps with electric lights, but he did not personally work in mines that made that change until after the 1930s. He also noted that from his experience the price of gold was the most important factor in western mining development during the Depression, but the silver subsidy certainly aided the industry.

Through the 1930s, the Reconstruction Finance Corporation (R.F.C.), which had originated under Hoover but continued with the New Deal, made loans to small businesses. By early 1934 the Washington office of the agency had received 5,000 applications for mining loans from small firms, and by 1938, several dozen western firms had received loans on average of $20,000, almost all of which were for gold. Several Alaska firms received larger totals.[37] In these secondary areas, the New Deal affected mining in much the same manner that it affected other major segments of the economy. However, the guaranteed government purchases of gold at prices greater than the free market clearly gave all gold mining a favored position. Walter Bradley summed up the advantage just after the gold price increase.

> Gold mining is one industry in which competition hurts no one; in fact there is, strictly speaking, no competition in gold mining, except possibly the rivalry of who can take out the largest chunk of it. Each dollar of gold added to the country's coffers does the work, today, of $10–$20 in the backing it gives to credit in the business and commerce of the world.[38]

With mining prospering, the Rocky Mountain region was one of the areas of the country least affected by the Depression, and federal dam construction and other programs also favored a stronger economy in the West. Further, mining received a subsidy, as mentioned, for *both* silver and gold with the final success of the free silver movement that had originated in the nineteenth century, but the subsequent massive inflation predicted by that movement, which was supposed to aid farming, failed to materialize.

Professionals

The guaranteed prices for gold and silver set by the Roosevelt administration in early 1934 profoundly affected the overall mining industry. The recovery of mining had begun with lode gold at approximately the same time as individuals in the automobile gold rush were moving into placer areas and for the same reason—profits. However, mining professionals made more permanent, long-lasting contributions.

Mining engineers, skilled miners, and prospectors all found themselves in demand. These were not amateur panners or even small businesses using Denver Gold Savers or other limited equipment. These were specialists who had spent years developing very focused abilities, either through formal education, as with geologists and mining engineers, or working in a variety of hard-labor occupations which often required more years of practical training than some occupations filled by college graduates. Underground mining necessitated great expertise in operating drills, setting explosives, and avoiding injury in the ever-changing conditions of a heavy work area hundreds or even thousands of feet below the earth's surface. Underground crews working in shifts might typically spend eight hours drilling a series of 16 to 20 holes in a definite pattern. By the 1930s engineering analyses could be used to determine the most efficient placement of the dynamite, which varied with particular rock types. At the end of the shift the crew put dynamite deep in the holes with long tamping devices and detonated the charges in a sequence usually beginning with those at the center of the cluster.

The crew on the next shift removed the broken ore and gangue (non-ore bearing rock) from the floor of the mine in the tough job of mucking, then loaded broken ore and gangue into ore cars. Some equipment could ease these demanding tasks, but only the larger mines could afford items such as mucking machines and electric locomotives. The process was then repeated again. Of course, conditions were continually changing, and techniques that worked well in one mine might not work in another. As workings went deeper, timbering or supports were required to prevent cave-ins. Workings could go in virtually any direction, depending on the appearances of ore bodies and the potential for finding better deposits. A hole might go straight down in a working called a winze (a task very difficult to perform) or it might go straight up in a raise (much easier since the broken rock could fall down). Various parts of underground mine workings have special names; the main work area where ore is removed is called a stope. Larger mines often had more specialization and designated particular workers as muckers, timbermen, miners, or by different titles for various outside jobs dealing with material transportation and processing.

Obviously, pneumatic drills, which could make a sufficient number of holes in just one shift, were a crucial technological improvement in mining in the 1870s, along with dynamite. Prior to these two inventions, mining had depended on *Black Powder and Hand Steel*, as mining historian Otis Young titled one of his books on the technical aspects of mining. By the 1930s these old methods might still be found in small, remote mines. Underground miners did not face the severe level of danger in the 1930s that they had in the previous century, but the occupation was still one of the most demanding and hazardous of any, and, unlike many professionals in other fields, miners had to deal with constant life-threatening dangers from equipment, explosions, bad air, or cave-ins. While underground, the miners' lives depended on proper timbering, good ventilation equipment, and well-maintained drills, and it took skill and experience to learn to avoid unexploded dynamite, which might still lurk in dislodged ore or vein faces. Gas pockets could also prove deadly.[1]

Those who worked underground were not the only mining professionals. The professional prospector also provided a great opportunity for human interest stories, especially if some major mining activity resulted. Chapin Hall, a reporter for the *New York Times* who went West in the 1930s, provided his version of a "generic" figure of the period: "This modern prospector differs from his prototype of the Fifties and Sixties. He does not wear whiskers, and he

Fig. 16—*Underground mining with a heavy pneumatic drill. The miners drilled a series of 15 to 20 holes, then set charges. This type of heavy industrial mining required considerable capital for equipment and years of experience among miners. The only appropriate term is professional mining.* Engineering and Mining Journal *133, no. 7, p. 10 (used by permission of Maclean Hunter Publishing Co.).*

rides in an automobile, but he is just as confident that he will soon have the long-sought mother lode in the bag." By 1933 Hall could see tangible results from the rising mining economy even as far away as Los Angeles. The stock exchange there was active in a number of mining-related issues, especially long-abandoned properties being

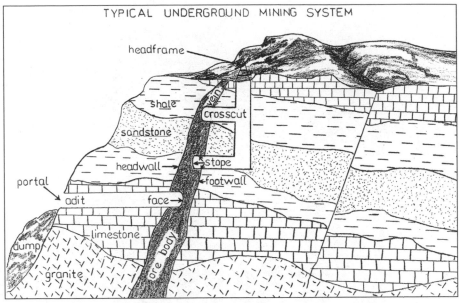

Fig. 17—Typical underground mining system. Drawing by Connie Miller.

returned to production. To support the many new ventures, $20 million in machinery and supplies would come from Los Angeles alone over the ensuing six months.[2]

In Idaho, the Orofino District (*orofino* is Spanish for fine gold) had long been an active gold locale as part of an extended region of central Idaho that had produced gold since the 1860s. The early summer of 1932 saw a revival of mining interest when prospector J.R. Crawford found what was described as a "free milling gold lode six feet thick." The thickness of the vein gave it an excellent return on the costs of working the find. Assay values ran as high as $1,110 per ton. That same summer a new vein was discovered in an existing mine near Pearl, Idaho, which brought $25 per ton and employed 14. This discovery justified construction of a new mill that used flotation processes and which had a capacity of 125 tons per day. The Mayflower Mine near the remnants of the town of Quartzburg had lost its mill in a forest fire that destroyed the town the year before. Gold profits justified construction of an innovative new mill which used more efficient crushing methods than traditional stamp mills.

Fig. 18—A small underground mine in Idaho which enters the ground through an adit, a horizontal tunnel or portal entry. Courtesy Idaho State Historical Society, Boise, Idaho, #63-160.3.

The new mill was designed by A. W. Fahrenwald, a professor at the University of Idaho.[3]

Idaho's ghost towns lived again, and in more areas of production than gold. At the once active community of Atlanta, the St. Joe Lead Company was spending $25,000 per month. Mountain Home and Silver City, long dormant, were prospering. The owners of the appropriately named Come Back Mine in the Boise Basin located a new vein 2,000 feet long and had soon developed a drift 900 feet into it at a depth of 200 feet. The ore assayed at 20 ounces of gold and several hundred ounces of silver per ton. As early as August 1932, Idaho's Secretary of State granted articles of incorporation to two firms that capitalized their new ventures with major outlays of $300,000 and $370,000. Another Idaho community, Elk City, had been historically productive but had declined almost into a ghost town while gold was undervalued. By early 1934, even before the increase in price to $35 per ounce, 21 mines had reopened there and were carrying a total monthly payroll of $17,550.[4]

Prospectors did, in fact, discover new mines in the early 1930s, much as they had in the previous century. However, as with the Idaho examples, the new mines were generally in locales or districts with producers known to have good potential nearby or on the same mining claims. The Whitney Mine near Mina, Nevada, resumed operations after 60 years. At the well-known camp of Goldfield, Nevada, a prospector named Heine Miller discovered a vein which brought $40 per ton of ore in mid 1931 in a long-worked shaft of a mine which had been explored many times. The most striking item about this discovery was the fact that Miller was blind.[5]

In the known Nuka District near Seward, Alaska, a discovery of a vein assayed at $50,000 per ton naturally brought a rush to that area. With the influx of prospectors, another major find soon resulted at the nearby Willow Creek District. Here a vein 14 feet in width yielded $45 per ton. And in mid 1932 at virtually the same time as those discoveries, two other prospectors near Cordova, Alaska, observed a receding glacier and noted that it had exposed a vein. Sure enough, the vein assayed as high-grade gold. Another rush resulted but the discoverers had already filed 22 claims on the most promising ground.[6]

Colorado provides another good example of successful professional prospecting. In that state, the primary mineral belt runs diagonally across several massive mountain ranges from the northeast, near the town of Boulder, to the southwest, with Telluride approximately at the far end. The general pattern shows more gold to the northeast, more silver to the southwest. However, ores may be found anywhere along the belt in a variety of combinations of gold, silver, lead, zinc, copper, molybdenum, and other materials. Tom Walsh's famous Camp Bird Mine near Ouray in the far southwest, for example, operated into the 1990s a gold producer. Activity in the early 1930s focused on the northeast end of the belt where production dated from 1859 with as many as 1,000 prospectors combing the area again in an effort to find another major strike.[7]

A discovery in the Silver Cliff area of Colorado brought enough follow-up to recall events in the nineteenth century. On May 12, 1933, prospector Robert Hoard of Cañon City, Colorado, found a rich vein. The Associated Press wire service reported Hoard's discovery, as did one of the first issues of a new publication titled *Newsweek*. Both stressed the fact that Hoard was a "Negro Prospector" and gave him just credit.

Hoard was not the first in the area to find pay dirt that spring; three others had been quietly working a nearby vein of their own, which assayed at $500 per ton. They were Ed Hollister, the state prison fingerprint expert, John Drake, a school teacher, and James Mow, a hardrock miner. They had been able to keep the discovery a secret for a profitable period, until Hoard had made known the presence of the valuable zone and brought a rush. The three miners who predated Hoard's arrival then hired guards to protect their possession. The A.P. story included this memorable passage:

> Bearded veteran prospectors and tenderfeet jostled on the rock-strewn wagon road into the upper copper gulch country where yesterday a Negro prospector, Robert Hoard, found paydirt which runs $38 to the ton . . . 250 autos [arrived] loaded with men and women . . . [and] a tent city sprang up overnight. Claims were staked for miles around. Squabbles over overlapping claims and claim jumping added to the excitement.[8]

This discovery in the areas of Westcliffe and Silver Cliff, Colorado, was particularly interesting since it was far from the state's primary mineral belt, though some ores had been found there since 1878. Elsewhere in Colorado, the only other major concentration of ore outside the primary mineral belt is at Cripple Creek, which is geologically different from those found in the primary mineral belt.

Fairplay and Alma, Colorado, stand near the northern end of the main belt. One of the zones of intense placer activity discussed in chapter 1 is in this area. Several large lode gold mines in the Mosquito District were present along the London fault and nearby London Mountain, and mining there had been continuous since 1872 but had fallen substantially in the early twentieth century. In 1931 the London Gold Mine was employing 120 miners who lived at a bunkhouse at the remote site. They produced 36,000 ounces of gold that year. The American Lode Mine, adjacent to the London, employed 40. In fact, the two mines narrowly avoided a court fight over the "apex rule," which allowed the owner of the top of a vein to claim the entire vein to its total depth.

The ore was moved out of the mines by railroad, bound for the mills at Leadville and Colorado Springs. In all of calendar year 1931, these mines produced a total of 470 freight cars of ore. By early 1932, trains of the Colorado and Southern narrow-gauge railroad had become too heavy for the diminutive antique steam locomotives to handle, and train crews had to drop cars to move the loads at all. A train of 16 cars proved too heavy even for two locomotives. By April 1932, the railroad dispatched three locomotives to move a train of 21 cars, but again the load was too much and one car waited for the next train. In one month alone—June 1932—the total number of ore cars ran to 134. That year the average monthly output of ore cars was 100, a rate that was still being maintained in mid 1935.[9]

The towns of Fairplay and Alma formed a regional supply center for the mines themselves, which were located in the surrounding mountains a number of miles away. However, placer operations did function at both towns. Everyday life was quite similar to small-town life throughout the country during this period. In the first half of 1932 there was one robbery of a store, one murder not related to mining, and a series of thefts of slot machines by a gang which simply ripped them out of businesses and escaped in a Buick. A particularly blatant slot machine theft brought a roadblock by the sheriff, but to no avail.[10]

An indication of a renaissance in Fairplay was the revival of the local movie theater, recalling Larry McMurtry's novel and movie *The Last Picture Show* about a dying small Texas town. The story ended with the movie theater going out of business. Fairplay had been in the position of seeing its only theater close a few years earlier. But by early 1932, when many other small towns across the country were losing theaters and a host of other small businesses during the deepest part of the Depression, mining made it possible for Fairplay to reopen its theater. The first new movie was "The Painted Desert," appropriately a Western with a mining theme. The feature film consisted of eight reels and tickets cost 20 cents and 40 cents.[11]

In spite of *Saturday Evening Post*'s Arthur H. Carhart's report of incidents of gunplay and claim jumping in this area, a thorough study of the Fairplay and Alma newspapers and those of Leadville, which was close enough to report major incidents, reveals only a few violent occurrences unrelated to claim jumping. In fact, this area had mostly been claimed many years earlier; now prospectors primarily focused on mineral lands already legally appropriated to private parties. In the mid 1930s Colorado had a total of over 45,000 mining claims which were fully patented, that is, privately owned. There were some legal problems for new developers in consolidating and clarifying legal possession. One mining man had to buy "129 sixty-fourths" of a certain area to ensure the title since various parties had overlapping claim boundaries. But none of these resulted in legal actions sufficient to draw the attention of newspapers in nearby small communities.[12]

There were still parallels, however, with mining camps from earlier times. After mines were generally established and providing good wages, the presence of a large population of single young males naturally led to the quick appearance of the common vices of gambling and prostitution. These social conditions had been present in virtually all mining areas across the West, both during the initial rush and for many years thereafter. Even today these activities arc legal, permanent parts of the overall economy in Nevada, and periodically have been in many other arcas as well.

These activities were less common among most poor placer miners. Though resident in many of the same areas, they had little if any money to spend on "vices." Moreover, they were often family men with families very much present.

In the desert areas of the Southwest opportunities for new discoveries were also present. Of course there had been mining in the region since the prior century. None other than Wyatt Earp and his wife Josie had prospected much of California and Arizona and had filed many mining claims. They worked ore at their best discovery, the Happy Day Mine, by themselves. This claim in San Bernadino County, California, dated from 1905. But they could not cover all of the huge region, nor could a mass of other prospectors.[13]

In the spring of 1932 the discoveries of some significant gold deposits near Yuma, Arizona, on the Colorado River drew national publicity. Placer gold had long been known along the river, but the locations of the veins that fed the placers had held their secrets for many years. The discoverer gave them the name the Santa Claus claims, thus adding to their news interest. United Verde Extension, one of the leading firms in the region, paid $30,000 for the claims, and the development prompted a reporter for the *New York Times* to view the event in much the same way that his colleagues had when reporting on common men placer mining. Edwin J. Wheeler wrote, "Old and young prospectors have again loaded the patient burros. . . . The spirit of the pioneers, which above all is one of hope, still rules in Arizona. For in gold prospecting the real lure is not what you get, but what you expect to get tomorrow, the next day, in the near future." Literally hundreds of prospectors were roaming the area; on just one day—April 14, 1932—they filed over one hundred mining claims. This again demonstrates the more professional nature of gold discovery at this point in time; amateur miners just squatted.[14]

Other sites in Arizona also had intense activity. At Castle Rock 25 miles north of Phoenix a number of amateurs worked along with one professional, J. C. Wheeler, who recovered as much as $8 per day, with an average of $3. He had a distinct advantage in his secondary trade; he could make the gold he recovered into watches and jewelry and sell them at his own jewelry shop in Phoenix.[15]

Similarly, at Quartzite, Arizona, in the far western part of the state, a number of amateurs lived in tents in early 1933 while one small professional firm dug a shaft. The gravels here were consolidated enough, and in such a dry climate, that some blasting was required to loosen them. At a depth of 90 feet in the shaft, the professional miners found a pay streak five feet deep worth $8 to $15 per ton. The firm was able to sell one pound of gold at $20.67 per ounce for a weekly gross profit of $336.72.[16]

Activity in the southwestern deserts spilled over the border into the Mexican state of Sonora, which was similar geologically and had a long history of mineral development. By early 1932, the twin cities of Nogales, Arizona, and Nogales, Sonora, were providing supplies to the Altar Valley farther south. Here many amateurs were working, but Ranon Elias, a professional with heavy equipment, was most successful. Significantly, $10,000 in gold was entering the United States weekly.[17]

Even farther south in Mexico at the same time, in the state of Sinaloa, a mob of prospectors engaged in pitched gun battles over claims. Violence as well as polluted water killed fully 60 percent of the participants in that local rush, as reported by the *Engineering and Mining Journal*. The entire event sounds very much like the unforgettable tale of greed described in *The Treasure of the Sierra Madre* written by a mysterious figure who used the pen name

B. Traven. In recent years Traven has been conclusively identified as a German named Ret Marut who gave another alias, Hal Croves, when, in 1946, he was an advisor on making the novel into a movie. John Huston directed the picture, and his father, Walter Huston, played the wise old prospector opposite a younger hothead played by Humphrey Bogart. Marut, who set his novel in Mexico, was certainly aware of the situation in Sinaloa, and may have felt justified in his view of humanity after observing the situation there. Though *The Treasure of the Sierra Madre* did not appear in print in the United States until 1935, it was first published in Germany in 1927.[18]

Gold also came into the United States from sources north of the border, just as had been the case with the Klondike discoveries in 1898. New finds at Atlin, British Columbia, and at the Great Bear Lake continued this pattern.[19]

Various contemporary sources disagreed as to whether or not prospectors wore beards or whether they all drove cars or whether they still used burros. Even the *Engineering and Mining Journal*, generally intent on showing the most up-to-date methods, found a photo of a prospector's burro irresistible and noted that the San Juan Mountains of southwestern Colorado were too rugged for wheeled vehicles. By 1935 some prospectors had even begun using washing machines to recover placer gold. Yet the message that a sense of optimism drove their very existence is inescapable in all of these stories. By the spring of 1933, G. M. Butler, the Dean of the Arizona School of Mines and head of the state's Bureau of Mines, estimated that 3,000 prospectors were searching the remote areas of that state alone.[20]

Arid Mojave, California, approximately 75 miles due north of Los Angeles, where there had been mining activity over many years, showed considerable promise for new ore discoveries. Here in the fall of 1933 prospector George Holmes discovered the vein that would become the Silver Queen. Holmes had found a "blind lead," by randomly blasting prospect holes. A blind lead is a vein with no outcrop or surface expression to give a clue as to its presence but which contains valuable ore at depth. One individual, Virgil Drew, owned a 20 percent interest in a claim in the area which he sold for $1,000 just before its true value became known, and a photo of his dejected countenance appeared in newspapers across the country.[21]

Map 3—*Scattered gold areas lie across the desert regions of southern California.* Engineering and Mining Journal *135, no. 11, p. 518 (used by permission of Maclean Hunter Publishing Co.).*

The discovery of the Silver Queen, which despite its name had high gold content, naturally drew more prospectors, developers, and a wide range of camp followers from throughout the West. Just over a year later, the A.P. wire reported from Mojave, California, that "George and Ralph Wyman drove in from the hills, the rumble seat of their roadster filled with ore . . . similar to the Silver Queen." The entire region became more active within another year as additional mines opened at Soledad Mountain and Mid Buttes near Mohave and Neenach. (The latter town is now a ghost town dating from the recent 1930s.) The region was close enough to Los Angeles to make food and other goods available at reasonable prices compared to more remote mining areas.[22]

By 1936 the area around Winnemucca, Nevada, experienced a significant lode rush which had several unusual aspects. Indeed, the *Saturday Evening Post* found enough potential in the development to dispatch a reporter for its first story on the automobile gold rush since 1932—Frederick R. Bechdolt, a veteran miner/prospector himself who went on to become a serious historian and writer on the West. Back in 1898 he had carried a 100-pound pack at least 20 times over the incredible "staircase in ice" of 1,200 steps at Chilcoot Pass on the trail to the Klondike in Canada's Yukon. (The Canadian Mounties required each stampeder to possess certain minimum pieces of equipment necessitating many climbs to assemble the gear.)

After crossing the pass, Bechdolt and the other stampeders had built boats and proceeded on an adventure down a wild river. Of all the gold rushes, the Klondike was perhaps the most demanding not only in terms of simply arriving at the diggings but also in subsequent survival in an arctic environment. He could not help but compare his personal experiences with those he found in 1936 Nevada where prospectors used "late model cars," and arrived over "paved highways." The differences in transportation formed one of the main thrusts of his entire report. The primary figure responsible for the activity near Winnemucca, the seat of Humboldt County, was unquestionably George Austin, who had lived in the area for many years. Austin and his wife had run a small ranch and hotel and had raised three children. Austin had spent many years prospecting across the region and had grubstaked a number of other prospectors. By the time of his success, he was in his 60s. J. C. Stagg and Clyde Taylor were two of the prospectors who Austin had backed, and they made a great discovery in early 1935. Austin, acting as a mining developer, bought the mining claims from these prospectors for $10,000 on the terms of $500 down and two years to pay the balance. As Bechdolt put it, "Under the skins both breeds are just the same; one works on top of the ground and the other beneath it but the driving motive is a deep-seated faith in hidden riches."

Austin quietly developed and worked the mine for 15 months, sending the gold to the U.S. Mint, as federal law required. No one beyond the immediate area realized the gold was coming from a recent discovery instead of longstanding mines. The story finally leaked when no less a figure than mining engineer and former president Herbert Hoover paid a visit. Then a throng of prospectors, developers, "mining engineers, and millionaires" arrived. Austin received an offer of $1 million from a South African firm but kept the mine. One other party, Standard Oil Co. of California, found some success with its nearby Jumbo shaft.

Bechdolt observed the clean, orderly nature of the influx in his *Saturday Evening Post* story. He saw no gambling or seedy camp followers, and he felt it was a significant enough point to observe that "three women in tents were prospecting with their husbands." This contrasted markedly with historic mining rushes and even with contemporary situations he observed in Nevada. However, Bechdolt arrived at the mines at Winnemucca at such an early stage that he got a distorted view. Even at the time of his visit there was already evidence of attempted claim jumping in the form of altered dates on the posted notices.[23]

In the Potosi District of Humboldt County, Nevada, two other prospectors discovered a new vein which became a profitable gold producer. A 1934 discovery by Emmet Chase and Ed Knight entered production in 1938 as the Getchell Mine and produced low-grade ore (i.e., ore having a low content of gold). However, the Getchell Mine contained tungsten and arsenical ores, which made recovery economically feasible, and this mine was permitted to remain open during World War II following the closure of other gold mines by the United States government. The Getchell Mine was the state's largest gold producer for several years and remains in production today.[24]

Almost all ores are chemically complex enough to produce important by-products in addition to recovery of a primary metal. Ores found in conjunction with gold and silver that could also be recovered often made the difference in whether or not a mine could successfully be reopened in the 1930s. Even before increased price supports in 1934, gold and silver found in combination with industrial metals such as copper, lead, zinc, and molybdenum could often bring in sufficient additional income to make a mine worth working. The situation only improved when higher price supports for gold and silver went into effect.

Cripple Creek, Colorado, along with neighboring towns also in the gold zone, had contributed greatly to the nation's recovery from the Depression of the 1890s. Geologically, this district differed from other mining areas since the ore-bearing veins consisted of gold-silver telluride minerals, which are markedly different in appearance from typical quartz veins, which contain particles of gold that are not chemically combined with the surrounding quartz. Telluride ores are consistently the same metallic material since they are a chemical compound. Beginning with the Pikes Peak rush in 1859, several generations of prospectors had combed the area, but the tellurides were not fully recognized until the 1890s. By that date it was only a short distance to major railroad and smelting facilities at Colorado Springs. Historically, $361 million of the entire Colorado total of $744 million of gold production up to 1934 came from Cripple Creek.[25]

By the end of 1934, after gold reached $35 an ounce, Cripple Creek's miners had produced a total that year of over $6 million. Just four years earlier the total had run to only $1 million. As a result of the price increase, the owners of two well-known mines employed 175 workers to drive a new tunnel from the 2,000-foot level of the Ajax Mine to the 2,100-foot level of the Portland. The district produced even more in the later 1930s with improvements in facilities and recovery methods.

Over 80 percent of Cripple Creek's production had gone by rail to the Golden Cycle Mill at Colorado Springs for many years. In 1935 502,000 tons of ore went to that mill, and in 1936 the figure was 40,000 tons more, but the district required even more milling capacity. By late 1935, the massive increases in ore production had justified an investment in a new $400,000 mill at Cripple Creek itself which included three major steel buildings, offices, scale, and dumping bins with a 500-ton capacity. Mines had descended as deep as 3,000 feet. Cripple Creek drained its mines of water with two tunnels built in the early twentieth century, but more drainage was needed. By 1939 several mines and the Golden Cycle Mill had constructed the Carlton Tunnel to drain shafts deeper than those sunk during the original rush period.[26]

The population of Cripple Creek reached 3,000, and, like Fairplay, Colorado, the residents decided to restore the movie theater. The town instituted a massive publicity movement and held a Donkey Derby on August 16, 1931, which attracted several thousand

Table 2. Lode Mines in California

Year	No. Mines	Employment	Employment per Mine
1929	538	6,374	13.8
1930	476	4,962	12.4
1931	640	4,453	8.7
1932	817	4,172	6.9
1933	973	5,511	8.1
1934	1,227	7,254	8.1

SOURCE: U.S. Bureau of Mines (S. H. Ash and Emory Smith), *Some Facts Affecting an Accident Prevention Program in Metal Mining in California*, Information Circ. 6909 (Washington: Government Printing Office, 1936), p. 3.

spectators from larger cities east of the Front Range. Despite a delay due to a hailstorm, the revenues from derby tickets sold for the race between 35 donkeys provided a "first-class movie house and talking picture machine."[27]

Since the 1850s, California's largest lode producers had been in a district which included the towns of Grass Valley and nearby Nevada City. In 1931 a new gold zone entered production at the 16 to 1 Mine. The largest single mine in Grass Valley was the Idaho Maryland, owned by the company of the same name, which produced approximately 21,000 tons of ore per month, contributing to the region's total of 75,000 tons per month. At Nevada City the Murchie Mine was the leader with 9,500 tons of ore per month. The total for the district in gross profits for 1933 was $3.8 million *in cash*, 80 percent from Grass Valley.[28] Another famous area on the Mother Lode, Calaveras County, saw important new lode development on Carson Hill.

The Bodie, California, district on the Nevada border far from the Mother Lode experienced the same increase in ore values that prompted new development, despite a 1932 fire which destroyed much of the historic area. A cyanide plant capable of processing 500,000 tons a year of tailings from old mines began operation in 1935.[29]

These larger California mines were exceptions to the general pattern along the Mother Lode, where many very small lode mines were active in the 1930s. However, professional skills were needed at small underground mines in hardrock locales as much as at larger mines. The many small mines made up for the lack of particularly large operations, as can be seen in the following table summarizing Depression trends in all underground California mines, not just gold producers. Even so, the importance of gold as a stable product and the impact of the 1934 price increase is obvious.

The *Mountain Democrat*, published at Placerville in the center of the Mother Lode, reported few placer activities during the initial amateur phase of gold recovery. But in early 1934, when the gold price increase became permanent, the paper initiated a regular section on mining activities, including information on a local Gold Miners' Club which held weekly meetings. Editorially the paper called for new highways and the opening of railroad lands under established mining laws and credited Roosevelt's price increase with the renewed interest in this historically famous gold region.[30]

A particularly large, interesting, and relatively little-known gold district was centered at Oatman in northwest Arizona and extended throughout Mojave County. Initial discoveries there dated from 1863 or 1866, but a major rush did not come until 1902, and a high level of activity continued until 1924. There was also a significant rush between 1916–17, a period contemporary with World War I, and most of the newcomers came by automobile at that time, making Oatman the center of an automobile gold rush many years prior to the more widespread trend of the 1930s.

The Tom Reed Mine had been a major producer from 1902, but discovery of a vein of ore that became the United Eastern Mine brought the first major rush of Model T automobiles. Since the new discovery was adjacent to the Tom Reed Mine and fell under the apex rule of the federal Mining Law of 1872, the owners of the Tom Reed sued. Resolution of the suit had huge financial potential, so the case went all the way to the U.S. Supreme Court. In this complex case the Tom Reed owners demonstrated that only one vein was present; however the United Eastern owners won in 1922 by successfully countering that though the vein dipped for some distance, it became horizontal at depth and hence the apex rule did not apply. Even so, the Tom Reed Mine had a longer life—the United

Eastern played out in 1926. By 1931, the owners of both were on much better terms and agreed to join the mines at the 1,110-foot level with a crew from the Tom Reed drifting east to make a connection. At this date, the Tom Reed was producing $100,000 per month. It remained in operation until World War II.[31]

South Dakota's Black Hills region included the famous Homestake Gold Mine near the town of Lead, as well as a number of smaller gold mines. The Homestake Mine, which had operated since 1877, was the largest single producer in the United States and could even compare with the large mines in South Africa. This mine alone provided an eighth of the United States' total gold production. When the price for gold increased, the Homestake more than doubled its production between 1935 and 1941 to over 500,000 ounces per year.[32]

Several historic mines in Montana showed renewed production. The Paymaster Mine brought a ten stamp mill to its site near Diamond City. It provided 12 jobs. The Vosburg Mines near Winston hit a vein at 200 feet which contained $22 of gold per ton. Several other mines near Helena were active. At Blackfeet City, the Victor Mine found a vein which assayed at $100 per ton. This vein was 13 inches wide at 750 feet, and was obviously a highly professional undertaking. The mine employed 20.[33]

A scattering of other lode gold activity shows the types of operations that were emerging during the early phases of the Depression. The Sutro Tunnel Corp. owned and operated the famous tunnel at Virginia City, Nevada, one of the most significant feats of mining engineering of the Comstock Lode period in the previous century. The firm developed other Nevada properties including the Crown Point Mine, which yielded an estimated $1 million in 1931.[34]

By the 1930s, companies could purchase state-of-the-art dredges for large-scale placer operations. In 1850, California became the first recorded site for use of a dredge when an imaginative tinker converted a steam-driven boat, the *Phoenix*, into a dredge, but it was not until the early twentieth century that dredging became a significant part of the gold mining industry. Local contractors often constructed dredges, fitting them to local conditions. However, a major San Francisco firm, the Yuba Manufacturing Co., became the leader in the field and served an extended area of California favorable for heavy dredge mining equipment. Most large dredges became known at that time as California-type dredges.

A dredge is essentially a piece of machinery that lifts materials from the bottom or bank of a waterway and deposits them elsewhere. Many dredges are used to clear channels for navigation or deposit waste materials elsewhere. In the case of gold dredges, the materials dredged also go through a series of screening, sluicing, and washing processes. The machinery then ejects waste gravel and sand back into the stream or onto a bank behind the dredge. Some types of equipment were misidentified as dredges but were instead floating washing plants. Such plants do not directly remove gravel from a streambed. Instead they use a separate earthmoving shovel or dragline, which picks up gravel and places it in the processing plant and then places the processed ore on the streambank.[35] Sometimes stone and gravel wastes left in dredge piles are recovered for use in construction; more often they remain even today as permanent, unsightly scars on the landscape attesting to the extensive history of dredging operations throughout the West.

The first California dredges were powered by steam engines, but in the 1930s, these were replaced with diesel- and gasoline-powered internal combustion engines. The internal combustion engines were also powerful enough to move a series of buckets along a continuous chain for digging out gravel and dropping the gold-bearing materials on the ship's deck for processing in a perpetual operation. Obviously, the volume of gravel that the equipment could process was only one key factor affecting profit margins; gold content of the gravel was the second critical factor.

Gold dredges often required construction of a dam to provide enough water to float the hull of the dredge so that it could successfully operate. However, the fact that the device was specifically constructed to move large volumes of materials gave it the ability to dig into new areas, allowing water to flow in from behind it. Most machines had an extremely shallow draft and could be used on many streams that carried low volumes of water. Locations favorable for dredging had generally seen considerable placer mining activity on a smaller scale, and the dredge mining companies would either acquire established mining claims in a given area or would pay royalties to the parties that legally owned the mining claims, as allowed under the federal Placer Mining Act of 1870.[36]

By the 1920s most California dredges constructed in the earlier part of the century had ceased production, and only 686 dredge miners were cited in the 1929 Census, reflecting the decline. Predictably, the increased price of gold dramatically boosted output, and by late 1934 California alone had ten areas where large dredging operations were successful—seven in the traditional Mother Lode area and the remaining three in northwestern California. There were a number of dredges operating in each of these ten areas. Calaveras County had four functioning dredges by 1937 which produced 17,469 ounces of gold or 54.1 percent of the placer total for the entire county. Four more dragline operations in Calaveras produced 7,762 ounces or 24.1 percent, and 42 other operations using smaller methods produced the rest. This distribution was generally reflected throughout California demonstrating the difference that large-scale equipment could make in placer recovery.[37]

Yuba Manufacturing produced the majority of dredges, either as new or reconstructed models. In one case Yuba remodeled a dredge that had been built in the early twentieth century and had last operated in 1926. This dredge returned to production in 1934 with a new steel hull 233 feet long, 68 feet wide, and 11½ feet deep. The dredge used 126 buckets to move river gravel, each with a capacity of 18 cubic feet. The new hull weighed 1,200 tons and the total weight of the dredge was 3,220 tons.[38]

In 1935, after the increased gold price generated even more interest in and capital for the mining industry, Yuba Manufacturing Co. produced a totally new dredge specifically for a site near Ione, California. This dredge featured 82 buckets on an endless chain and was capable of moving 7,300 cubic yards of gravel per day. It had a hull 88 feet by 40 feet with a draft of 7 feet. Instead of using steam, gas, or diesel, this dredge was "all electric" and operated by drawing power from a heavy power line that paralleled the streambed.[39]

By 1935 Yuba Manufacturing had been so successful that it brought out a model named Yuba Junior, a smaller standardized dredge weighing 110 tons and having a capacity of 800 cubic yards per day. The more compact size allowed smaller streams to be worked profitably.[40]

Yuba Manufacturing didn't have a monopoly on the manufacture of dredge equipment. Between October 1934 and January 1935, the Natoma Mining Co. constructed a new dredge for a site six miles west of Folsom, California, for $400,000. This dredge had a massive capacity—12,000 cubic yards per day—and used a 500 h.p. engine to run 62 buckets each with a 16-cubic-foot capacity. The steel hull was 114 feet long, 54 feet wide, and 11 feet deep. This huge machine owed its existence to the increased price of gold in 1934. Many others would follow, until World War II stopped gold mining dead in its tracks in 1942.[41]

Some dredges weighed more than a seaworthy vessel, though the configuration of the machinery made them top-heavy. At least three in California capsized. The first was a very large dredge, the Natoma Mining Company's no. 8, which sank on April 29, 1935, near Folsom, California. This particular dredge had operated since 1913. It had a hull 150 feet by 56 feet by 10 feet and a capacity of over 14,000 cubic yards per 24-hour day of operation. The firm righted it and sold it for component parts. In late 1937 a smaller Oroville Dredging Co. machine capsized on the Feather River. A restoration project finally refloated Oroville's in the spring of 1941 at about the same time another California dredge capsized—the huge Tuolumne Gold Dredging Co. machine worth $600,000. In none of these cases were there any casualties.[42]

California was not the only locale in the West where large and small dredges could operate. Just north of the state line the same placer zone evident in northwestern California stretched into southwestern Oregon. Two dredges and five floating washing plants were in operation by 1941. A dredge in the Black Hills of South Dakota recovered $1,000 in just three runs of six hours each. After this success, several other firms formed to begin dredging in that famous gold region where hundreds of more ordinary miners were also attempting to survive. In Montana, an area on Meadow Creek above McAllister attracted a $50,000 investment for a dragline as early as 1932. Estimates of 50,000 cubic yards of material with a recovery rate of $.50 a yard drew the investors' interest. One large dredge of 7,000 cubic yards per day capacity operated on Gold Creek in Powell County, Montana, in 1934, while a "dragline and stacker scow," with a capacity of 1,500 cubic yards per day, operated on Prickly Pear Creek near Helena. Still another operated at Virginia City, Montana, a classic placer area northwest of Yellowstone National Park. In 1939 two other new dredges of medium capacity entered production in Montana, one at Prickly Pear Creek, the other at Washington Bar.[43]

In Idaho, dredges were first introduced in the 1890s, and gold production from dredging attained an all-time high between 1932–42. Several dredges were operating in the gold regions of central Idaho by 1935, and these areas produced a total of 23,850 ounces of gold—a more than 50 percent increase over production in 1934. On Jordan Creek in Owyhee County, a medium-sized washing plant with dragline processed 3,000 cubic yards per day. This particular operation began in 1937 and worked gold tailings dumped into the creek many years earlier by the DeLamar Quartz Mine. Other Idaho dredges operated at Warren, Pierce, near Elk City, in the Boise Basin, in the Hoodoo district of Latah County, at Owyhee, and in other areas of the state.[44]

Even states generally thought of as too arid to support dredging had some places with significant placer deposits and enough water to justify trying to recover placer gold in this manner. In the arid state of Arizona, Lynx and Big Bug creeks in the Prescott area combined sufficient water and enough gold-laden gravel to support major dredging operations. The Calari Mining Co. operated a dredge 50 feet long, 35 feet wide, and three stories high on Lynx Creek that could circulate an average of 3,000 gallons of water per minute, but they had to build a dam on the stream to impound enough water to permit a machine of this size to function. During the spring of 1933, in 61 days it processed 60,000 cubic yards of gravel which yielded $.32 per yard. A dragline shovel with 1½ yard capacity fed the dredge, which also worked on its own to a depth of six feet below the streambed. The operation required a total of twenty workers on three shifts. Subsequently the Lynx Creek Placer Mining Co. used two draglines and a "floating washing plant" to process even larger volumes of gravel in the same area, specifically 556,115 cubic yards in 1938 and 542,815 cubic yards in 1939. Unfortunately, no employment figures are recorded, but the value of the operation is evident.[45]

Another dry state, Nevada, had sufficient gravel and water near Tonopah to justify a substantial dredge operation owned by the Manhattan Dredging Co. and constructed by the Pan American Engineering Co. of Berkeley, California. This dredge used jigs 42 inches by 42 inches, which gave it a 12,000-cubic-yard per day capacity (jigs employed slightly cupped devices that moved through the water).[46]

Alaska Territory naturally possessed physical and climatic condi-

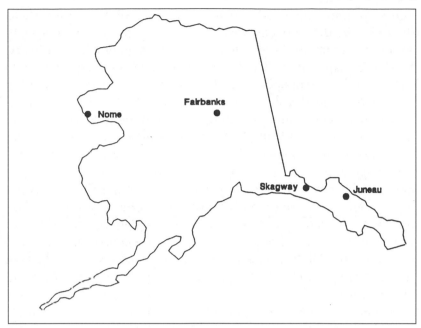

Map 4—Alaskan locations historically associated with gold mining.

tions that were virtually the opposite of the desert areas of the Southwest. Even so, it was similar to the Southwest in the basic fact that a harsh environment made dredging, and all placering, a technical challenge. However, the availability of water coupled with the extent of deposits ultimately proved most profitable. Because of the remoteness and the technical difficulties, the amateur stage of the mining boom of the 1930s had essentially by-passed Alaska. Professionals filled in the void early and became even more significant after the final gold price increase to $35 per ounce in 1934. In 1936 a survey of 15 operators revealed an average 130-day season, but this could vary widely depending on local conditions and climates. One large locale of placer gold was on the Seward Peninsula in the west-central area and included the famous town of Nome. The largest gold deposits were in the Yukon Valley, which includes Fairbanks. However, several other regions also had considerable production.[47]

Unquestionably, the dominant firm in Alaska was the United States Smelting Refining and Mining Corp. (USSR & M), which figured prominently in other regions and types of mining as well, as discussed in the next chapter. In Alaska, USSR & M undertook some operations in its own name and some under its subsidiary, Fairbanks Exploration. The firm's developments by 1938 reveal its success and scope of operations. For some years it had attempted to mine a rich but deeply buried streak near Fairbanks on Cripple Creek (not to be confused with the lode mining town of the same name in Colorado). Finally, USSR & M installed the largest walking dragline then in existence, with a bucket of 12 cubic yards' capacity. The dragline traveled along the bank removing 10 to 50 feet of upper barren gravel. A huge hopper device carrying the processing equipment ran on tracks in the excavated area, and the dragline dumped materials into the hopper for processing. In 1940 USSR & M introduced a new dredge in the same locale constructed at a cost of $1,000,000. All these major pieces of machinery were products of Bucyrus-Erie, a well-known manufacturer of many types of heavy equipment.[48]

Nome, with its heritage of an earlier gold rush, naturally saw renewed activity. There, too, USSR & M dominated the field but certainly had no monopoly. Many gold deposits were in salty ocean water rather than fresh water, with the resultant corrosive effects on hulls. In 1931 one dredge had worked over the gravel in its area so the owners moved it nearly two miles across land, then refloated it in another prospective area. A serious fire wiped out much of the town of Nome in September 1934, just as had happened in many classic mining towns in the prior century. Even so, gold production continued, just as it had after the earlier fires.[49]

Elsewhere in Alaska, Miss Gladys Comstock worked a claim 40 miles from Juneau for three years and traveled to her placer area by airplane. She made enough to pay for a vacation in the Far East and drew an Associated Press story. Near Valdez, a firm led by Clarence W. Poy, described by the *New York Times* as a "Chinese-American mining engineer," leased a known gold property, the Big Four claims, in a deal significant enough to draw another Associated Press story.[50]

Alaska's total production figures and their implications are staggering. The Territorial Commissioner of Mines, B. D. Stewart, issued comprehensive reports every two years, which reveal the magnitude. In 1934 at $35 per ounce, total production was 457,343 ounces or $16 million gross, but the physical volume was much the same as it had been the year before and would remain so the year after. Some 30 dredges contributed $6.7 million of that total. By 1940 production stood at 725,000 ounces for $25,375,000. Dredges alone accounted for almost half of the total. All placer mining employed 4,240 with 1,905 of those working on 52 dredges, 1,380 on draglines, and the remainder on smaller ventures. With an average recovery of 55.8 cents per cubic yard, the richness of Alaska's deposits and value of their development are obvious, despite the difficult environment. Clearly placer mining was king in Alaska, the only jurisdiction where this was true, but lode mines were still important. Some 123 underground gold mines employed 1,957 workers in 1940.[51]

For further comparison, the total population of Alaska in late 1929, when the official U.S. Census took place there, was less than 60,000 and slightly over 50 percent of these were Alaskan native peoples. By late 1939 the population was 73,000, of whom 39,000 were listed as white. Of course, many more people came to Alaska during the summer months for seasonal employment such as fishing, canning, and lumbering, as well as mining. The Census dates were specifically selected to get a count of more permanent residents after the seasonal workers had left. Even so, the 1940 total of nearly 6,300 engaged in gold mining alone during the warm months represented perhaps 20 percent of the total work force and was by far the most of any jurisdiction under the authority of the United States.[52]

Conditions in Colorado were much more like Alaska than other stateside areas because of the state's generally high altitude, which led to many mining concerns like working a shorter season and having to deal with heavy snows. In Colorado one dredge had operated on the Middle Fork of the South Platte River near Fairplay since 1922 at an elevation of nearly 10,000 feet. At least two operated at Breckenridge in the 1930s. Here the dredging firm found it economically viable to remove part of the older section of the town because it rested on gold-bearing river gravel. These same locales had drawn many down-and-out miners in the 1930s, as the *Saturday Evening Post* had reported.[53] Ironically Breckenridge today is a glamorous, wealthy skiing resort. Artifacts left by earlier miners who resided there are now considered quaint items that give the town local color. One large dredge has been remodeled to serve as an exclusive restaurant, and meals cost more than what the original miners received in a week's pay.

There were many more types of dredging equipment operating across the United States than those mentioned, but the ones cited give a good idea of relative sizes and capacities. However, three huge dredges that entered production in Colorado merit special mention. All three began operation in 1941, the last year of mineral expansion prior to World War II. Component parts for the largest dredge arrived by truck from the Yuba plant in California and were delivered to a site near Fairplay that spring. When completed, it was to have 103 buckets with a capacity of 11 cubic feet each and be capable of digging 70 feet below water level. It dug right into riverbanks ahead of it, which were as much as 35 feet above water level, so in effect it mined 105 feet from ground level on the bank to below water level. The hull was 158 feet long and 54 feet wide; total weight was 2,524 tons. It required a crew of 24. Though the hull and bucket dimensions as well as the total weight were smaller than a few older dredges noted above, it had a distinct advantage in its 1,500 h.p. General Electric engine.

Prior to installation the builders anticipated the dredge would have a capacity of 17,000 cubic yards per day, but this estimate proved to be very conservative. South Platte Mining Co. initiated operations with it on June 11, 1941, and the dredge processed as much as 5 million cubic yards per year, though it was out of operation for a period during World War II. By 1952 it had processed and reprocessed 33 million cubic yards of materials that yielded a total of 115,000 ounces of gold—over 3½ tons—for a gross profit of over $4,000,000, but in the end its machinery only recovered $.06 of gold per cubic yard, an extremely low return considering the costs of running the dredge. Subsequently the dredge sat abandoned until 1980, then it was dismantled and shipped to a mining area in South America. This dredge at Fairplay, Colorado, and its two sisters, which were also of substantial size, represented state-of-the-art placer mining by processing a huge volume of materials.[54]

The favorable economic situation had a notable impact on college graduations of professionals entering mining engineering and related fields. The four or more years necessary for graduation delayed the immediate impact, but the numbers of graduates from the prestigious Colorado School of Mines at the town of Golden near

Fig. 19—Yuba No. 17 was touted as California's largest gold dredge "which was able to work to a depth of 150 ft. below the surface." Engineering and Mining Journal 135, no. 11, p. 486 (used by permission of Maclean Hunter Publishing Co.).

Denver show an undeniable pattern, which reflected the improved opportunities in the field of mineral development.

All Colorado School of Mines graduates were in one of four fields: mining engineering, metallurgical engineering, geological engineering, or petroleum engineering. The commencements for each year from 1931 through 1937 averaged exactly 79 at the bachelor's level. As late as 1934, the class numbered only 70. Further, the school awarded a scattering of graduate degrees, and a special honorary degree to former mining engineer and former president of the United States, Herbert Hoover, in 1935.

Graduation of 1938 was especially interesting since 46 of the 99 undergraduates had finished their degrees in 4 years without interruption. Given the time frame, this group had entered college in the fall of 1934, when the Silver Act was just giving mining a long-term favorable economic outlook. The average age of this class was 23.5 years. In the very next year, 1939, the School of Mines awarded 131 bachelor's degrees, far surpassing the old record of 108 back in 1923 (which itself was anomalous since it reflected a large group delayed by World War I). Graduation of 1940 saw 144 receive undergraduate diplomas with seven more receiving graduate degrees. And 1941 had 155 march to the strains of "Pomp and Circumstance" for bachelor's degrees with three master's and two doctorates. In every class,

approximately half of the graduates were from the State of Colorado, the remainder from other states with a scattering from foreign countries.[55]

For overall comparison, throughout the U.S. the undergraduate
college level enrollment had been 1.08 million in 1932 and had risen
to 1.39 million by 1940. Bachelor's degrees awarded across the land
increased from 138,063 to 186,500 over the same interval. Thus the
powerful jump at the Colorado School of Mines of over 100 percent
between 1934 and 1940 clearly reflected economic trends beyond
population growth or the rising educational level in the country.[56]

So what jobs could graduates with degrees in mining related
fields command? Obviously, a wide range of enterprises hired the
majority. However, professional government agencies also hired a
number. The various state agencies as well as the U.S. Geological
Survey and the U.S. Bureau of Mines presented the best prospects
for newcomers in the field. Chapter 1 included discussion of various
guidebooks for amateur miners. However, the agencies had found
those relatively simple to compose. The highly technical reports required by professional miners were far more demanding of the
highest skills of field observation and laboratory research. A notable
paper which appeared early in the decade addressed gold in Idaho
and was a cooperative effort by that state's Bureau of Mines and the
U.S. Geological Survey. Many subsequent reports showed similar
cooperation, though state and federal agencies also wrote many
studies by themselves.[57]

A final observation on professional as contrasted with "amateur"
miners is in order. The WPA research team that prepared the detailed report on placer miners attempted to show a connection between spectacular newspaper stories and the arrival of people
unprepared for the reality of the situation. They noted that stories of
spectacular lode strikes by professional prospectors added to this
psychology. Certainly, it is understandable that such an interpretation arose.

One only has to look at the California State Fair as well as county
fairs. Along with displays of farm animals and crops, these fairs included exhibits of spectacular placer gold nuggets. One finder en-
trusted a nugget of 38 ounces to Walter W. Bradley for exhibition at
the 1934 California State Fair. Another display at the El Dorado
County Fair won first place for the entire event. Idaho responded by

displaying spectacular nuggets from the Boise Basin. Naturally the average person could see such exhibits and be enticed to go to the gold fields. However, these exhibits were actually the work of professionals who had the equipment to move huge masses of materials. Some spectacular nuggets would eventually appear; the question was how much other material had to be processed to get to them.[58]

Despite news stories and even tangible exhibits of gold nuggets, relatively few of the ordinary people who took up placering expected a dramatic return. Of course, they could always hope. Today, the presence of many state lotteries attests to a similar psychology. Yet when questioned, the typical buyer of a lottery ticket will admit the chances are one in millions. However, some income was to be made in mining, and for those with developed skills in hardrock techniques, the returns were the best of any industrial occupation in the Depression.

Silver and Spin Offs

Even though gold had been a main reason for an increase in interest in mining in the early 1930s, overall the mining industry was still economically unstable. Silver prices had fallen from $.53 per ounce to only $.28 between 1929 and 1932, and production had fallen from 61 million ounces to 23 million. Copper collapsed from $.18 per pound to $.05 during the same period, and volume fell from one million short tons to less than one quarter million.[1] The abysmal prices of silver, copper, lead, and zinc drove out smaller firms and idled many skilled miners. Underground mining, however, was so specialized that only a few workers had enough experience to master the required skills, and many gold mines in the early 1930s employed men who had previously worked in silver, copper, or lead/zinc mines.

Sharlot Hall, a prominent figure in Arizona society and politics, wrote to M. F. Westover on June 17, 1932, revealing the human element affected by the drop in copper prices.

> The closing of the copper mines has thrown thousands of people out of work and half the towns in Arizona are like abandoned places. All winter people went away if they could go and struggled to get into California and the warmer regions of southern Arizona.
>
> They begged for food and for gasoline to keep going—many of them having cars of some sort—and the little local settlements were just swamped as with a retreating army in war time.
>
> Now that it is warmer they are spreading out into the hills and mountains in the hope of placer mining and getting a few cents a day out of the gravel bars that were worked over fifty

years ago. Sometimes they really do pan out a few cents—or
once in awhile they get a dollar or more—but the old diggings
are very lean of gold—having been worked over all these years
(Sharlot Hall Archives, Prescott, Ariz., Sharlot Hall Collection,
item 1, File Folder 15, Doc. Box 1).

The silver price rise of January 1934 saw many mines with historically high silver production reopened, and the silver bill increased
confidence that prices would remain high. The Bullard Mine in central Arizona was sold when the bill passed Congress for "an undis-
closed but substantial sum" even though it had been idle for over 50
years. Its purchase was newsworthy enough to be mentioned in the
Arizona Republic.[2]

Another mining area with a long history, Mercur, Utah, saw revived activity brought on by the Silver Purchase Act. When the bill
passed in June 1934, another operation in Utah also found that it
could profitably move high-grade ore even with mule trains, as had
been the case in the prior century. At least two localities long known
as ghost towns in Idaho—Silver City, which dated from the 1860s,
and Mt. Chance—had crews at work of 100 and 40 respectively by
mid 1934.[3]

Classic locales where silver was found are scattered across the
West. Virginia City, Nevada, was among the best known, and Colorado had famous Leadville and the extended San Juan region con-
taining a number of medium-sized silver centers. The Coeur d'Alene
area of northern Idaho was another significant extended region.
Lesser areas included Park City, Utah, and Tombstone, Arizona.

A row of famous mines lined the Main Street of Virginia City,
Nevada, and the adjoining town of Gold Hill. Each of these mines
marked the original claims filed according to local mining laws when
the massive silver vein was first recognized in 1859. Subsequently,
major financial interests consolidated the mines as districts ma-
tured. Most of the mines had closed by 1886 because of high costs
associated with depth of the mines (reaching nearly 4,000 feet), the
high rock temperatures at those levels (about 160 degrees Fahren-
heit), and the large quantities of water encountered. Today each of
Virginia City's historic mines is still remembered by a local street
name. By 1933 the Arizona Comstock Co. was mining part of several
of the most famous original mines including the Hale and Norcross,

the Chollar, the Potosi, and the Savage, but high costs caused their closure in 1938.

Adjacent to these was the first major producer in pioneer days, the Ophir, which took its name from the Bible, specifically I Kings 9:28 and I Chronicle 29:4. The original Ophir was the lost mine of King Solomon, and many mining districts across the West had mines named Ophir. In late 1933, discovery of favorable ores deep in Virginia City's Ophir Mine led to new activity, and mining crews blasted exploratory tunnels (often called crosscuts) to the west, back toward the mountain that overlooks Virginia City, rather than away from it, as the pioneer miners had done.

Though Virginia City never returned to the glory days of the previous century, some production did come from the historic mines and there was also some new development. Much the same was true at the White Pine and Reese River Districts, near the Nevada towns of Ely and Austin. These two areas began production in the 1860s, soon after Virginia City, and became major mining camps, but were not as well-known.[4]

Leadville, Colorado, had a nineteenth-century history just as colorful as Virginia City's past. At Leadville, a flamboyant group of millionaires and stock manipulators had openly tried to surpass the activities of Virginia City's mining clique. The most famous was H. A. W. Tabor, who became the focus of one of the most notorious scandals of the century when he divorced his wife of many years to marry Elizabeth McCourt Doe—known as Baby Doe—a much younger woman.

Leadville had a particularly violent reputation as a mining camp during its heyday in the late 1870s through the 1880s, with frequent robberies, murders, and vigilantism. In the 1930s Leadville was still predominantly a silver center, but it had enough gold in the early 1930s to show some signs of fortune. Like other silver camps, it started the year 1934 on an upbeat note with the rise in silver prices to 64.5 cents per ounce. In April 1935, the price rose to 77.5 cents per ounce. Profits from silver production in Leadville thus rose from $700,931 in 1934 to $842,996 in 1935 even though this 20 percent advance came from the same physical volume in ounces. A new mill of the Ballard Gold Corp., with 1,000 tons capacity, began operations on Breece Hill in the main mining area just east of the town itself.[5]

Map 5—Major hardrock mining locales across the Rocky Mountain States.

In June 1934, the public school system conducted a census. Adults numbered 3,026 compared to 2,762 exactly one year earlier. Individuals aged 6 to 21 numbered 1,334, up from 1,253, and infants through age 6 numbered 427 compared to 367 at the same time in 1933. The improved economic climate clearly caused population increases. During the same period, the total assessed value of real estate for all of Lake County rose from $5,697,000 to $5,839,335.[6]

Leadville was a fairly typical small town of the 1930s. During 1934 and 1935, when Leadville was experiencing its greatest boom in half a century, there was only one shooting incident that resulted in an arrest. The typical resident had a much greater chance of serious injury or death in a mining or railroad accident. During the two-year period, there were three recorded deaths of workers in mines and smelters and three suffered serious injuries while there were two fatalities and 17 injuries related to railroad accidents. And the leading cause of injury and death in twentieth-century America appeared in Leadville—seven died and seven were injured in automobile accidents.

The death of Baby Doe Tabor by natural causes drew nationwide notice, and a hoard of reporters arrived after neighbors discovered her remains on March 7, 1935. She had lived in a cabin at the Matchless Mine since the early part of the century supposedly because she was following the advice of her husband, who had believed the mine still held valuable ore, though Duane A. Smith, Tabor's biographer, cites evidence to dispute this tale.[7]

It is interesting to compare life in Leadville in the 1930s with life there in 1880 when, from March to mid September, there were 18 deaths from shootings, five suicides, six fatal accidents, one killed by whiskey, and a number of others who died with no cause listed. During the last three months of 1880 some 34 persons were jailed for murder, making Leadville one of the most violent towns in the West, but it also had a population then of over 14,000.[8]

Leadville in the 1930s can also be compared to another town of the 1880s that had virtually the same total population—Bodie, California, which was at its height from 1877 to 1883. U.C.L.A. history professor Roger McGrath surveyed Bodie (and nearby Aurora, Nevada) in *Gunfighters, Highwaymen, and Vigilantes* (1985) and identified many violent incidents in those towns that were recorded in contemporary newspapers. Stagecoach holdups were frequent and vigilantism emerged. For the seven-year period there were 31 shot, stabbed, or beaten to death and 14 committed suicide—six women and eight men, and this in a community with a ratio of men to women of ten to one. The women were particularly prone to abuse alcohol and opium, dependencies that frequently led to suicide.[9]

In the San Juan Mountains, southwest of Leadville, several other smaller silver towns had similar frontier backgrounds and conditions in the 1930s that were much the same as at Leadville. The return of ore development followed the pattern evident at Leadville. Near Telluride several major mines reopened that had been important in the 1870s and early 1880s, most notably the Liberty Bell, Tomboy, and Smuggler-Union. The latter had been one of the most famous mines in the Rocky Mountain West. With higher silver prices, even tailings left at these mines proved valuable, and one firm employed 24 people to rework them. Another significant mine, the Black Bear, which dated from 1898, sold at the end of 1934 for a price of $1 million, a figure later raised to $1.5 million when the additional costs of restoring equipment were added in. In July 1935 the Telluride mines sent 35 cars of ore via the Rio Grande Southern Railroad to smelters at Leadville and elsewhere. A full census is not available, but in 1934 elementary school enrollment was 121, up from 94 in 1933, while high school enrollment was 54, up from 50.[10]

There appear to have been few disputes regarding claim jumping or other boundary overlaps primarily because most mining was in locales which had seen earlier production. However, the occasional new discovery in a locale with few prior mining claims led to problems. The La Plata Mountains of far southwestern Colorado had seen generations of prospectors but relatively little development. In June 1933, two prospectors, the Starr brothers, recognized a gold vein of oxidized ores in surrounding sedimentary rock. This occurrence was so unusual that the U.S. Department of the Interior even submitted a press release to explain the geological circumstances. The brothers founded Red Arrow Corp., began development, and turned a substantial profit. Predictably, other prospectors rushed into the area, and although no other discoveries resulted, within a year the Starr brothers were embroiled in a serious lawsuit filed by another prospector, H. L. Whipple. The fact that similar situations did not occur in previously developed areas is indicative of the overall maturity of the industry.[11]

Another interesting mine developer in Colorado was a young engineer in his twenties who in 1935 was on the verge of completing a bond and lease deal on two silver mines he intended to work. When his partner and backer died unexpectedly before the deal closed, Robert A. Heinlein went on instead to become a professional writer whose several dozen imaginative science fiction books sold more than 40 million copies over the next 50 years. Heinlein had graduated from the Naval Academy in 1929 and had become an engineering officer, but a bout with tuberculosis forced him to leave the Navy in 1934 and move to the dry climate of Colorado at the very time silver was booming. Though he never worked the Sophia and Shively lode mines, his passing interest in mining has been compared to a similar phase in the career of the great American writer of the prior century, Mark Twain. Much of Heinlein's personal background, including his origins in Missouri and an affinity for the frontier, was indeed quite similar to Mark Twain's, and biographer Leon Stover contends that Heinlein was simply a later version of Twain who placed his picaresque tales in a future setting.[12]

Still another extended region famous for silver since the previous century was the Coeur d'Alene Mining District in northern Idaho, which showed an overall economic improvement that paralleled, or even exceeded, the Colorado silver areas. For example, the Hecla mine in northern Idaho was the primary producer for the Hecla Corporation. Hecla operations included mining silver, lead, and zinc. A sharp rise in their profits between 1934 and 1935 resulted primarily from the government's Silver Purchase Act setting the price of silver at $1.29 per ounce, as well as an increase in the price of lead. In the second quarter of 1934, profits had been $38,981.44; second quarter profits in 1935 were $265,661.22.[13]

Mining was the most important employer in the Coeur d'Alene area in the 1930s, but the timber industry, agriculture, and even tourism were also significant. The town of Coeur d'Alene in Kootenai County served as the regional commercial center in the 1930s and was the home of the region's daily newspaper, three radio stations, two movie theaters, and a wide range of retail outlets. Most of the miners and their families lived in the smaller towns of Wallace and Kellogg in nearby Shoshone County, but the economy in both counties relied on mining in one way or another. Lumbering, for example, was partially based on the production of mine timbers from forests and sawmills.

Severe labor strife in the last decade of the 1800s, which carried over into the first decade of the twentieth century, had left the Coeur d'Alene region with a colorful and violent reputation and a place in the history books. A dispute in mid 1892 over unionization ended after a pitched battle between union and nonunion workers. In the melee, the Frisco Mill collapsed after the union men set dynamite. There was one fatality in that incident and other fatalities from gunshots. Governor Norman B. Willey declared martial law and called up troops, which resulted in a management victory on wages, but the unions did see an end to the monopolies held by company stores and boardinghouses.[14]

In 1899 much the same pattern recurred, marking the climax of a tumultuous decade. A contingent of union miners commandeered a train and rode through the district vandalizing the facilities of mining firms along the way and dynamiting the $250,000 stamp mill at the Bunker Hill and Sullivan Mine at Kellogg. One nonunion miner was murdered, and Idaho Governor Frank Steunenberg declared martial law and secured regular federal troops to enforce it. These actions essentially broke the then dominant union in Idaho, the Western Federation of Miners.[15]

More violence related to strikes in the Coeur d'Alene region continued. On December 30, 1905, retired Governor Steunenberg died in a dynamite trap left at his front gate in Caldwell in southern Idaho. Local authorities soon arrested Harry Orchard, a known hoodlum, and he implicated the leadership of the Western Federation of Miners, even though the union's focus was then in Colorado. Colorado officials literally railroaded union president Charles Moyer and union secretary-treasurer "Big Bill" Haywood to Idaho on a special train late at night. This proved to be a public relations disaster for the authorities, although the U.S. Supreme Court upheld Idaho's right to try the men once they were in Idaho. Haywood was tried first and the trial drew reporters from around the world. William E. Borah, later U.S. Senator from Idaho, gained his initial fame for the prosecution while Clarence Darrow stood for the defense. However, the state could not produce evidence corroborating Orchard's story and Haywood was not convicted. Subsequently Moyer also "walked."[16]

The Western Federation of Miners had changed its name to the International Union of Mine, Mill, and Smelter Workers about the time of World War I, but was still unable to overcome its radical image following the violent events in the Coeur d'Alene District as well as in Colorado, where the governor also called up the military to end a rash of bombings. Big Bill Haywood contributed to the radical image of the union by openly declaring himself a communist and defecting to the Soviet Union. Some of the International Union of Mine, Mill, and Smelter Workers encouraged an openly socialistic if not Marxist stand, which led to the infamous Bisbee deportation in Arizona in 1917. Local authorities loaded some 1,700 suspect miners on trains and simply dumped them in New Mexico. This event became another public relations disaster for the officials, and even President Woodrow Wilson expressed disgust. However, the deportation did thwart the union at Bisbee, and subsequently organized labor virtually collapsed throughout the West. By 1933 the union had only six locals with 1,500 members, most of them in Montana but none in the Coeur d'Alene area.[17]

The advent of the New Deal and federally sponsored elections held under the auspices of the National Labor Relations Board gave rise to unionism again, particularly in the Coeur d'Alene region. Many workers had been afraid to organize for years because employers openly intimidated those who did, and the Coeur d'Alene mining area seemed especially ripe for organization when the National Labor Relations Board conducted elections in June of 1934. Even the local newspapers predicted a union sweep.[18] However, the results proved surprising.

The Federal Mining and Smelting Co., which owned two smaller mines, the Morning Mine and the Page Mine, did not even oppose the union. The work force at one comparatively new mine that showed great potential—the Sunshine Mine—voted pro union by 187 to 41, but the older mines recorded much closer votes. The Hecla favored the union but only by 194 to 178, and the largest mine in the region, the Bunker Hill and Sullivan, which had been the scene of the most destructive events of the 1890s, voted it down by 549 to 475, though the work force at the Bunker Hill and Sullivan finally did join the union in 1942.[19]

By mid 1935 all but one of the Coeur d'Alene mines were offering wages according to the following schedule: miners $5.25 per day, muckers $4.75, outside workers, $4.50. The one mine that did not follow this schedule was the Sunshine, which offered its workers $.50 more. However, these wage increases were not enough to hold the labor force of 3,000. A year and a half later, in early 1937, the Coeur d'Alene companies raised their schedule to $6.75 for timbermen, $6.25 for miners, $5.75 for shovelers (muckers), and $5.50 for common labor. The Sunshine continued to give $.50 more than the others in all categories.[20]

Mine workers in northern Idaho needed only to observe the outcome of a walkout against copper giant Anaconda in the neighboring state of Montana to realize their own good fortune. On May 8, 1934, the International Union of Mine, Mill, and Smelter Workers called a strike against Anaconda, which was then primarily mining under the town of Butte but had some outlying mines and smelters.

Butte had been one of the few locales where the union had remained active prior to federally sanctioned elections. Anaconda paid $4.25 per eight-hour day in 1934. The union leadership proposed a raise of $1.20 per hour with a 30-hour week and asked for a vote of the workers in support. Of 5,000 union workers only 1,500 showed enough interest to participate in the vote, which favored the strike by 11 to 1.[21]

The strike dragged on into August until a federal mediation team drafted a proposed settlement to take effect following a favorable vote of the miners. They would return to work at the old wage of $4.25 per day; however, if copper prices rose to $.09 per pound for a 30-day period, wages would increase by $.50 per day. Further copper rises to 11.5 cents per pound and to $.13 per pound would each bring wage increases of $.25 per day. In case of copper, if there were price decreases below these thresholds, the miners would continue to draw the old wages for six months before the scale reverted to the lower level. The miners accepted the settlement by a vote of 2,573 to 1,105 in September.[22]

Anaconda's copper miners had lost over four months in wages and returned at their old pay rate. Copper prices remained below $.09 through 1935 but rose enough to give the miners the first raise in 1936. In 1937 prices peaked at over $.13 but then collapsed below $.10, and the raises never did not come close to justifying the time lost in 1934. The strike seems to have been pointless. Perhaps the leadership believed that the silver price increase, then becoming permanent through the final law, justified their demands. However, the fact that almost all other copper areas, including Arizona, had been shut down since mid 1932 should have been a factor. The union was lucky that it did not lose the earlier pay scale.

The Coeur d'Alene miners used another criteria for evaluating their wages in the overall context of the times. The first minimum wage law signed by President Roosevelt in 1938 mandated $.25 per hour with a 44-hour week allowed without overtime. In 1940 the minimum went to $.40 per hour for a 40-hour week without overtime.

Miners in the Coeur d'Alene District and elsewhere generally avoided the labor disputes that marked such industries as automobiles, rubber, and steel at the same time largely because the mines paid well—especially if they produced gold or silver. However, even copper miners were fortunate by 1930s standards.

The Sunshine Mine was able to pay higher wages than other mines in the area simply because it had the best ore with the highest silver content. The other mines had large contents of lead and zinc, which were not subsidized. As early as June of 1934, before the Silver Purchase Act had time to be a factor, the mine declared a $240,000-dollar dividend or $.16 per share. The total profit for the previous quarter had been over $2 million, directly attributable to Roosevelt's price increase, which, as noted in chapter 3, had been made before the final act passed Congress in December 1931. The next month the mine shaft had been sunk to 2,300 feet and a new high-capacity mucking machine was being used. By November, the Sunshine had proven that an ore body was present to 3,000 feet depth with an estimated 650,000 tons of ore added to the previously known reserves in the mine.[23]

With a bonanza in silver in 1934 and after, the economy of the entire Coeur d'Alene region was virtually the antithesis of the stereotype of the Depression. In 1934 alone, the region added two new grocery stores and even a major new Montgomery Ward department store in the town of Coeur d'Alene, a town which found it could afford to spend $400 on a spectacular Fourth of July fireworks display.[24]

Shoshone County grew from a population of 19,060 in the 1930 Census to 21,230 in 1940, while Kootenai County went from 19,469 to 22,283. This regional increase of nearly 13 percent stands out markedly when compared to the overall increase throughout the country of slightly over 7 percent throughout the decade. Comparatively between 1930 and 1940 copper centers such as Butte fell from 39,532 to 37,081; neighboring Anaconda, Montana, fell from 12,494 to 11,004; and Bingham Canyon, Utah, dropped from 3,248 to 2,834. These declines would have been much worse without the silver subsidy.[25]

The patterns in the Coeur d'Alene area and Butte over time are ironic. During the economic hard times of the 1890s, silver prices were low and this was partially a cause of labor violence in northern Idaho. Copper prices were not as depressed, and two competing firms at Butte provided a demand for skilled miners which was very much to the miners' benefit. The contrast with the Coeur d'Alene area could not have been more dramatic. In the 1930s it was Butte which experienced the only serious labor dispute in western hardrock mining, in large part because copper prices were now low. Northern Idaho had wages that were among the best for skilled workers in any trade and busy mines. However, the comparison goes only so far. Butte's strike of 1934 was mild compared to Idaho strikes in the 1890s or Colorado strikes in the early 1900s. As recently as 1932, strikes in coal mining regions in the East and Midwest resulted in fatalities and a call-up of troops, much as in earlier periods of labor history. Further, the dispersal of the Bonus Army of World War I veterans by a regular army force under none other than General Douglas MacArthur became a national disgrace that same year. Though not in mining, the dispersal of the Bonus Army by regular U.S. Army troops fitted the stereotype of ordinary working men abused by the government. The 1934 copper strike stands out markedly since it ended not with federal troops but with federal mediators.

Lesser-known areas also profited from the revival of silver. Park City, Utah, had been active in the late 1860s through the 1890s until the greatest conflagration in Utah history destroyed almost the entire town on June 19, 1898. Thomas Kearns had come to Park City in 1883 and prospected and developed the Silver King Mine, which made him a millionaire. Kearns went on to become the first non-Mormon U.S. Senator from Utah and built a stately mansion on North Temple Street in Salt Lake City, which his widow donated to the state as the governor's mansion following Kearns' death in 1918. The Silver King Mine, Park City's largest, closed with the silver collapse in May of 1932, but the Silver Act of 1934 caused it to reopen in late 1935. By the 1950s Park City was almost a ghost town again (largely due to the costs associated with removing water from the mines), but like a number of Colorado mining camps, it experienced a rebirth with the introduction of skiing in the 1960s and today it is a popular year-round resort.[26]

Tombstone, Arizona, differed considerably from other silver mining centers in the technical problems that it faced. The largest group of underground mines began to experience water problems as early as 1883. Huge Cornish pumps to help drain the mines had been used successfully for some years, but the entire complex finally flooded in 1909. Labor problems at the same time compounded the difficulties, and by the early 1930s there was little mining activity. Despite the Depression the town was able to survive due to tourism. In 1929 a special event known as Helldorado celebrated Tombstone's wild west image and attracted national attention. The *Tombstone Epitaph,* the area's famous newspaper from the early days, featured historic human interest stories in an effort to capitalize on the town's past and dutifully reported on the scant mining activity that continued. Despite the flooding, a number of outlying mines were still operable and could be renovated. The American Smelting and Refining Company (now ASARCO) began to plan for revival as early as June of 1933 on property the company owned, and American Smelting built a new office building that fall.[27]

When silver prices increased in 1934, the *Epitaph* reported the entry of another major Utah-based firm into the area, none other than the United States Smelting, Refining and Mining Co., which was so active in Alaska. As early as March, activity was ongoing on 23 different mining properties and by October the total had climbed to 32. These were mostly leases to work existing mines. A firm from Mexico had the lease to work the Lucky Cuss while various Arizona firms held most of the rest. Other famous mines in renovation included the Last Chance and Toughnut. In mid 1934, over 300 miners were employed, certainly a favorable situation compared to 1932 when there had been none or even the prior year when there had been only about 150. There was enough activity to generate freight loads of ore. For the month of October 1934 the entire district produced 42 cars. The most reliable producer was the Empire Mine, which by 1935 was generating 18 cars of silver ore per month alone for the El Paso, Texas, smelter with a value of $1,000 per car.[28]

Money was flowing in Tombstone, and one of the town's best restaurants raised the price of its special Sunday dinner from $.40 to $.50, a large price jump for 1934. Tombstone's population fell from 849 in 1930 to 822 in 1940, but silver prevented a massive loss like the decline in neighboring copper-based Bisbee, where the population dropped by 27 percent below the 1930 total during the same period.[29]

Copper was the metal hit hardest when industrial demand collapsed. Through 1932 the market price averaged only $.05 per pound, compared to $.18 in 1929. The fact that copper mining provided far more jobs than gold and silver mining compounded the tragedy. Most major Arizona copper mines closed in mid 1932.[30] In 1929 copper had employed over 39,000 of the nearly 60,000 hardrock miners in the West. They had produced ores which yielded almost exactly one million short tons of finished metal in 1929, a figure which had dropped to 190,000 tons in 1933.[31]

Another measure of the collapse of copper was the price of stocks of major mining firms which had heavy holdings in that ore. Between September 1929, prior to the Great Crash, and September 1932, when the market had reached its lowest, various stocks collapsed.

Kennecott	88 7/8 to 13 5/8
American Smelting	121 to 18 ¾
Phelps Dodge	65 ¼ to 7 ¾
Anaconda	125 to 12 ¾
Miami Copper	44 to 4 1/8

Anaconda's corporate losses were typical—the company had a profit of $18.8 million in 1930 and a loss of $3.1 million the next year.[32]

There was a chain reaction throughout the economy. The Arizona state commissioner of property taxes cut the assessed valuation of all mining property in the state by slightly over 50 percent from a total assessed value of $243.8 million in 1931 to $121.5 million in 1932. The Arizona Bureau of Geology strongly endorsed this cut simply to keep firms in business at all and in a position to recall workers when prices improved. Other large businesses, including railroads and telephone and telegraph firms, also received some cuts but these were not as extensive as in mining.[33]

Another indication of the depressed condition of the copper market came from the Mormon church (officially the Church of Jesus Christ of Latter-day Saints). At the church's annual spring conference in Salt Lake City in 1932, Church President Heber J. Grant endorsed a protective tariff excluding copper imports from foreign sources. Ironically, in the 1850s Brigham Young had tried to deter mining because he feared the lure of gold might seduce church members into pursuing worldly instead of spiritual goals and mining might attract non-Mormons to Utah.[34] Mining development in Bingham Canyon southwest of Salt Lake City was delayed until finds in 1863 attracted the notice of Brevet Major-General Patrick E. Connor, then colonel of the Third California Infantry, a volunteer group based at Fort Douglas during the Civil War and charged with guarding the Overland Mail Route. Connor is known today as the Father of Utah Mining and was so taken with mining that he continued to pursue the development of mining properties in Utah and Nevada until his death in 1891.[35]

By the late nineteenth century, the Mormon church had come to realize that mining was a very important part of Utah's economy. Small claims were consolidated by larger companies into operations that relied upon cheap labor provided by foreign immigrants, making Bingham Canyon an ethnically diverse area. In the 1920s, the narrow canyon in the Oquirrh Mountains had a population of 15,000, and Utah Copper Company (later Kennecott Corp.) found the ore complex could be profitably worked at what has come to be today the world's largest open pit copper mine. In 1932, though, Utah, like Montana, Nevada, and Arizona, found itself having to deal with unemployment, collapsed valuations of mining properties, and all the related problems.

The boost that higher silver prices gave to copper cannot be quantified, but all copper mining regions began to show signs of recovery prior to official enactment of the Silver Purchase Act. By mid June 1934 stock prices had advanced considerably beyond late 1932 figures.

Anaconda	12 ¾ to 16 ¼
American Smelting	18 ¾ to 53 ¾
Phelps Dodge	7 ¾ to 18
Kennecott	13 5/8 to 23

By comparison, most major industrial and transportation firms had made recoveries since the low of 1932, but they were not as dramatic. The Atcheson, Topeka, and Santa Fe Railroad advanced from 54 to 62, U.S. Steel from 42 to 43, Standard Oil of California from 27 ¾ to 32 ¾, National Cash Register from 12 5/8 to 18, and Baldwin Locomotives from 8 to 11 ¾. The benefit of silver subsidies to mining were evident on the stock market, and mining stocks were even higher by late 1935. Most other major firms remained at their mid 1934 level or even lost ground. The rising prices helped total tonnage production peak at 841,998 in 1937 before falling back to 557,763 in 1938.[36]

Gold and silver by-products added to the improved economic picture for copper. Massive copper deposits are usually mesothermal deposits and were formed at an intermediate (not shallow) depth within the earth's crust. Above the mesothermal deposits had been higher-grade secondary copper sulfide deposits. At Bisbee, these had included higher-grade oxidized copper ores, but those were gone by 1903. Some of these locales had also been silver producers, since silver ores were often found in epithermal veins higher in a mineralized complex. Silver City, New Mexico, had even obtained its name from such a situation. By the 1930s, though, all the relatively shallow, high-grade silver was long gone, and profit margins dictated removing the growing masses of low-grade ores with copper dominant but with some silver as one of the by-products.

In an interview on January 18, 1997, Jim Bazzetta of Morenci, Arizona, described how his father, an Italian immigrant in the early twentieth century, had come to work in the mines in Arizona during the Depression. The recovery of copper aided by silver kept his father in a decent enough job as a skilled miner for him to afford a 1924 Dodge and allowed his son to finish high school in 1937 and subsequently graduate from the University of Arizona. Clearly this demonstrates the effect mining subsidies of the 1930s had on ordinary working families.

At Bisbee, Arizona, the first open-pit mine at Sacramento Hill produced ore in 1921 but was worked out by 1928. More ore would subsequently come from the large Lavender Pit nearby. By the 1930s, open pits had become important in the overall industry, though even in Arizona the majority of copper miners still worked underground. An exhibit at the 1933 Chicago World's Fair proudly and correctly advocated open-pit copper mining as the wave of the future.

In 1931, Phelps Dodge Corporation absorbed its rival in the Bisbee District—Calumet and Arizona—when copper was in the doldrums. There had been considerable recovery by 1935, but a strike idled 72 out of a total of 1,100 workers at Bisbee. The great majority of miners had seen the result of the strike at Butte the previous year so they took a different course.[37]

The giant Anaconda Corporation later became a leader in the open-pit method in its mines in Chile but had not done so in the early 1930s. However, the Montana areas were well situated for such development, and Anaconda excavated several open pits over the general region where underground mines had operated for years.

Other metals followed the same pattern. Lead and zinc, often found together, had been as low as 2.65 cents and 2.275 cents per pound, respectively, in 1932. By the start of 1937 they were up to 6 cents and 5.45 cents per pound. The largest lead/zinc deposits are scattered through the Midwest, but considerable recovery also occurred in the West. Mercury prices had accelerated dramatically for a flask of 76 pounds—from $47 in the fall of 1932 to $100 by 1937— as a result of the Spanish Civil War, which made world supplies quite unstable since the Almaden Mine located in Spain was the leading producer. The United States produced about a third of the 25–35,000 flasks the country used annually at the New Almaden Mine south of San Francisco, and the mine profited accordingly with the price increase as world supplies declined.[38]

The outpouring of ores required transportation. A number of major rail lines in the West were household names in the 1930s, including the giant transcontinental—Union Pacific, Southern Pacific, Santa Fe, Great Northern, and Northern Pacific. In addition, three medium-sized lines, the Burlington, the Denver and Rio Grande Western, and the Western Pacific, allied to form a transcontinental route connecting Chicago to California by way of Denver and Salt Lake City. All of these handled some ores along with smaller lines, which owed their survival to the mining boom then feeding into major systems.

Almost all railroad locomotives were steam powered in the 1930s; indeed many still ran even on transcontinental lines well into the 1950s. The transcontinental lines had modern designs and many of them used large Mallet engines with four sets of cylinders for long hauls over steep grades across the West. The small feeder lines were often still running the most antique equipment imaginable. A few of these once active systems still survive and are ridden by tourists and railroad buffs.

Among the feeder lines in Nevada were the Tonopah and Goldfield, Tonopah and Tidewater, Virginia and Truckee, and the Nevada Northern. The last connected the great open pit mines at Ely to the Southern Pacific and Western Pacific railroads. The Ely mines alone required 30 steam locomotives to move cars from the open pits with many more needed to connect with the mainline. Arizona had the Verde Valley, the Verde Tunnel and Smelter, the Ray and Gila Valley, the Tucson, Cornelia, and Gila Bend, and the Magma Arizona. Here, too, copper justified the lines' existence.

Colorado had a particularly interesting system since the extremely rugged mountain terrain required the use of narrow gauge (3 feet between each railhead) instead of standard gauge (4 foot 8½ inch) track. The Denver and Rio Grande Western remained the leader in miles of narrow gauge, even though it had converted its main lines to standard gauge some years earlier. Also, the Rio Grande Southern and Colorado and Southern were important feeder lines of narrow gauge. A fire in 1937 at the Colorado and Southern roundhouse at Como, just east of Fairplay, destroyed two locomotives and caused the abandonment of a feeder line in that area. An impressive number of narrow gauge lines still operated in Colorado in 1940, with some surviving into the 1950s. Outside Colorado, the only narrow gauge trackage of note was a branch of the Southern Pacific in California and Nevada, again a feeder to mining areas.[39]

The revival in all phases of mining naturally brought a revival in smelting ores. Copper mines dealt with such huge volumes of ore that it was usually more economical to place smelters near the mining areas. Other ores demanded other processes. Each mine required the development of an economical, technically feasible process for separate stages of smelting the output. To accomplish this task, mining engineers developed a flow chart to account for each stage of ore processing (see Fig. 21).[40] A mill for crushing ore was usually at or fairly near the mine while other processing, including smelting, was sometimes more remote. Ores of gold, silver, lead, and zinc were usually smaller in tonnage than copper, and it was often more economical to transport them to locations near fuel sources, or labor and market locations. Smaller mines often sent their ore over large distances simply because certain smelters could process their ores while others could not. Custom mills or custom smelters could handle various types of ore.

American Smelting and Refining Company unquestionably held first place in processing ore in the mining industry. Meyer Guggenheim had acquired several companies in the early twentieth century and had gone on to build an international smelting empire; the Guggenheim family still controlled the company in the 1930s. The

Fig. 20—*Colorado and Southern 2-6-0 Number 6 at the Denver engine terminal roundhouse in 1937. The Colorado and Southern Railroad abandoned much of its narrow-gauge trackage soon after this photo was taken. Other narrow-gauge lines in Colorado survived the 1930s because of mining. Several lines operate today due to tourist and historic interest. Courtesy Colorado Historical Society, Denver, Colo.*

first years of the Depression forced American Smelting to curtail many of its operations, including closing a plant in November 1930 that had operated at Durango, Colorado for many years. When smelting began to recover, the firm was able to accommodate all the ore that was offered. In addition to a venerable plant at Leadville, American Smelting had 14 other custom smelters in the United States and more in Latin America. Some American Smelting operations in the West were at San Francisco, Denver, Omaha, E. Helena, Montana, El Paso and Amarillo, Texas, and Hayden, Arizona. Each of these treated specific ores.

Colorado Springs had the independent Golden Cycle Mill, discussed in the previous chapter. The Salt Lake Valley had two American Smelting plants, one for copper and one for lead and zinc, plus the Kennecott smelter near Bingham Canyon, and the United States Smelting, Refining and Mining Co. (USSR & M) lead smelter at Midvale. The huge smelter at Midvale handled ores from great distances as well as nearby Bingham Canyon and Lark, Utah. It had operated since 1902 but had abandoned refining copper in 1907 af-

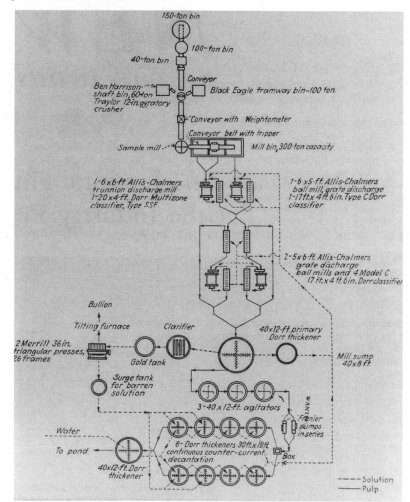

Fig. 21—Flow chart for the Tom Reed Mine, a major gold producer at
Oatman, Arizona. Engineering and Mining Journal 137, no. 5, p. 251
(used by permission of Maclean Hunter Publishing Co.).

ter a series of lawsuits regarding air pollution in Salt Lake City and
treated only those ores with high lead content. To control air pollution, the plant used a set of long cotton bags which were then
cleaned to yield another by-product—arsenic for weed killer.

In 1926 USSR & M expanded the Midvale facility by adding a
new mill that used a flotation process for lead recovery. In 1931 the

firm closed its plant at E. Chicago, Indiana, and concentrated its lead refining capacity at Midvale, and the nearby community was one of the few to experience a building boom in the depths of the Depression (though admittedly it was to the detriment of the environment). With the new capacity, the firm did very well during the recovery of western mining in 1934 and after.[41]

USSR & M's stock had sold for $52 per share just before the infamous crash of 1929. The price had fallen to $15 by late 1932. With the silver price guarantees, however, stock soared to $100 per share by September 1933 and $133 when the Silver Act passed in June 1934. Though the market in general, and mining in particular, had a good recovery during this period, USSR & M's was dramatic. Bullion worth $250,000 left the smelter on a variable schedule several times a month by armored car; deputy sheriffs and company employees guarded the cars with machine guns.[42]

The recovery in mining in the 1930s had a wave effect on manufacturers of tools and equipment. Many of these companies, which were mainly located in industrial states in the East and Midwest, began improving and modernizing their equipment, and the impact of the improved mining industry was felt in quarters well outside of actual mining regions.

Mining magazines and journals sprouted new advertisements. The few advertisements they carried in the early 1930s featured antiquated equipment such as carbide lamps, a chemically-powered miner's helmet lamp that had appeared in the early part of the century. Electric lamps powered by large belt-mounted batteries became the industry standard in the later 1930s. These were far more than simple flashlights, and the miners could use them for eight hours at a time and recharged over the alternate shift. Such equipment was also part of a new emphasis on safer working conditions and prevention of diseases, like silicosis, associated with mining. Mine Safety Appliances Co. of Pittsburgh, Pennsylvania, offered a wide range of emergency equipment including breathing apparatus, inhalators, dust respirators, gas detectors, and safety goggles. Larger equipment could now also be run from batteries, and underground mines installed battery-powered locomotives to move trains of ore cars. Firms that specialized in these items included Atlas Locomotive Co., in Cleveland, Ohio, Jeffrey Manufacturing Co., in Columbus, Ohio, and General Electric.

Industrial pumps of many descriptions had long come from and continued to come from the Worthington Co. of Harrison, New Jersey. Hoists came from Allis-Chalmers of Milwaukee. Drills, crucial devices in underground mining, came primarily from Ingersoll Rand of New York City. However, two other firms provided competition—Chicago Pneumatic Co. in New York, and Gardner-Denver in Quincy, Illinois. Mine car loaders came from Sullivan Machinery Co. Explosives came from Hercules or DuPont, of Wilmington, Delaware. Milling equipment came from Deister Concentrator Co., Ft. Wayne, Indiana. A wide range of other machinery items was available from Walworth Co. of New York. Even a leading cotton company, Mt. Vernon-Woodbury Mills Inc., advertised its products for filter cloths used in flotation plants.[43]

As late as 1934 none of the mining equipment suppliers were advertising in mining journals but all were doing so by 1937, and a large secondary market in used and refurbished equipment had also sprung up. The improved economy within the mining industry and its economic effects spread far beyond the western region and the firms which were directly engaged in ore removal.

The overall impact of the changed economic climate in mining is reflected in the figures released by the U.S. Census, which can be directly compared to those of ten years earlier. Though the Census officially occurred in 1940, the questions regarding income, employment, etc., reflected the prior year, 1939, while the Census of 1930 had similar questions for 1929.

In 1939 some 17,279 workers put in 40,842,000 man hours at mines specializing predominantly in lode gold. These mines employed 1,612 salaried workers. In 1929 "dominantly lode gold" operations had employed only 5,887 miners. Some 820 different firms with 841 mines and 329 mills provided these jobs. In 1929 there had been only 184 active mines "dominantly lode gold." Consequently, total wages for lode mines had risen from $8,655,505 to $26,931,219 over the decade, while the pay of salaried employees had risen from $1,131,247 to $4,003,971.[44]

According to the official U.S. Census of 1940, placer gold output totaled $28 million, with 339 mining properties of 306 firms employing 3,228 wage earners plus 477 salaried individuals. The wage earners' total pay came to $5,631,362; salaries came to $1,161,732. None of these figures included any firms which had less than $2,500 in machinery, buildings, or other equipment, thus many small miners, even those with several Denver Gold Savers or equivalent devices, were excluded.

Despite these omissions, the Census Bureau estimated that it had accounted for 97 percent of national production by volume and income. In comparison with 1940, the 1929 figures had shown only 37 mines employing 686 individuals for a total pay of $1,129,851. The increase, then, in workers was 458 percent over the ten-year interval. Broken down by state in 1939, as shown by the following table, California had the majority of placer mines, twice the number of operations and employees as all other states added together. (Alaska is not included since it was not a state until 1959. Sources cited in chapter 4, however, list 1939 placer employment there at 4,200, of which dredging employed 1,905.)[45]

Unfortunately, the tables do not separate dredging from other placer methods, but there is no doubt that dredging provided the bulk of production noted in 1939, just as it had in 1933. And the 1939 figures were gathered prior to several of the largest dredges going on-line over the next two years.

The number of active silver mines increased from 74 to 163 with

Table 3. State Placer Gold Production, 1939

State	No. of Mines	No. of Firms	Total Employment
Arizona	4	4	30
California	199	171	2,782
Colorado	21	21	119
Georgia	3	3	15
Idaho	27	23	240
Montana	30	29	283
Nevada	16	15	146
Oregon	28	30	295
Washington	6	6	24
New Mexico	4	4	25
Wyoming	1	1	6

SOURCE: U.S. Dept. of Commerce, Bureau of the Census, *Sixteenth Census, 1940, Mineral Industries*, vol. 1, pp. 345–50.

wage earners rising from 2,593 to 4,244. Salaried employees rose from 220 to 368. Those listed as proprietors increased from 25 to 85. Total value of production rose from $8,157,263 to $19,715,727. However, the Census officially noted that only 48 percent of the total silver production came from those mines "dominantly silver." Copper mines produced fully 21 percent and lead and zinc mines produced 18 percent while gold mines produced 11 percent.[46]

Overall, then, the western hardrock mining industry was about as well off in Depression year 1939 as in the last year of the roaring '20s. Though employment and profits from copper, the leading metal by volume, were down, as was lead, these losses were generally compensated for by rises in gold and silver. The overall industry was well-equipped and staffed and was quite able to quickly shift back to industrial metals again when faced by the emergency of World War II.

As with the amateur miners discussed earlier, professional mining interests also found that the western United States still had considerable potential. Undiscovered mining bonanzas did, in fact, remain to be found and worked. More significantly, classic districts like Virginia City, Leadville, and Cripple Creek, still held considerable quantities of ore. This situation, too, was something of a testament to the frontier school interpretation of the western experience and its potential to aid the overall national economy in a depression and to provide material in a world war.

SIX

Giants' Return

In 1848, the first wave of California placer miners used the simple equipment discussed in chapter 1—gold pans, long toms, rockers, and sluice boxes. The introduction of dredging described in chapter 3 gave greater access to gold-bearing gravel, but many stream banks were too thick or gold-bearing soils located too far from streams for dredging equipment to effectively process materials. Miners were tantalized by less accessible areas that were obviously laden with gold. As early as 1853, three veterans of the original gold rush, Eli Miller, Anthony Chabot, and Edward Matteson, an inventive Connecticut Yankee, constructed the first prototypes of what became the basic tools of hydraulic mining. By the 1870s the method had become widely used. Very powerful pumps directed a stream of water at a riverbank, breaking it up and releasing the gold-bearing gravel. The gravel ran downstream into large sluiceways which worked like regular sluice boxes but on a grander scale. Instead of small riffles, the sluiceways often used railroad ties to catch the gold. The pumps, usually known as Little Giants, constituted a major financial outlay. The Little Giants resembled a large fire hose nozzle or the even larger nozzles found on fireboats. Construction of sluiceways, local impounding dams, and sometimes ditches and flumes for water to supply the pumps compounded the expense. The water supply had to be at a higher level than the pumps so that there would be sufficient flow and this often entailed complex engineering and ditch and flume construction.

Hydraulic mining required relatively few workers, but the process recovered at least as much gold during the 1870s and early 1880s as the amount taken by hundreds of thousands of '49ers using small-scale equipment during the first two decades of California gold mining—an estimated $200 million or more.[1]

By the 1880s, hydraulicking was provoking legal and political battles in California because of the masses of water debris flowing downstream from the workings into the Yuba, American, Bear, Feather, and other rivers. These streams are tributaries of the Sacramento and San Joaquin Rivers, which water California's excellent agricultural lands. The extra runoff overflowed the river channels depositing masses of sand and mud and severely damaging some very productive farming areas. Pebbles, cobbles, and other heavy debris collected in riverbeds, and by 1880 the water level of the Sacramento River was seven feet higher than it had been in 1849. Only those riverboats with very shallow drafts could navigate even the largest rivers.

Both river transportation and farming interests opposed hydraulic mining, and the entire issue entered the courts, ultimately going to the U.S. Circuit Court of Appeals. Along the way, evidence was introduced in a mass of trials that 100 million cubic yards of gravel and clay had been washed into the rivers after 1876. By 1880, some 39,000 acres of agricultural lands had been destroyed and many more partially damaged, costing an estimated $3,250,000. In 1880, a severe phase of flooding deposited boulders and a damaging yellow mud known as slickens deposits. The 1880 floods alone "seriously injured" 15,200 additional acres.

How large was the source of the debris? In the early 1880s, approximately 500 hydraulic mines were operating and they required 6,000 miles of ditches for water supply to the pumps. The Little Giant pumps, and similar models such as the Monitor pumps, had nozzles eight to nine inches in diameter and could deliver 185,000 cubic feet of water per hour at a velocity of 150 feet per second. Total hydraulic equipment investment amounted to over $100 million, with some of the largest individual mines investing as much as $3 million. Annual mine production ran to at least $10 to $12 million, and possibly more, through the 1870s and early 1880s. Significantly, approximately 600 million cubic yards of gold-bearing gravel remained to be worked.[2]

Finally, the court set a major precedent on January 7, 1884, in the case of *Edwards Woodruff v. North Bloomfield Gravel Mining Company et al*. This became commonly known as the Sawyer Decision

Fig. 22—Hydraulic mining in California with a Little Giant pump. The use of hydraulic mining returned in the 1930s. Engineering and Mining Journal 138, no. 10, p. 31 (used by permission of Maclean Hunter Publishing Co.).

because Lorenzo Sawyer was the circuit judge who helped issue the decision. Though farming interests are often cited as the plaintiffs, the actual litigant, Edwards Woodruff, was owner of a shipping firm which had been damaged when rising waters had rendered the plaintiff's steamboat landing on the Yuba River at the town of Marysville, California, useless. In fact, the entire town of Marysville had been flooded in 1875 when levees broke and it had flooded again in 1881. It was also noted that ten to 15 feet of debris had accumulated above the old river bottom making navigation difficult.[3]

The court's decision favored the farmers as much as the riverboat firm by prohibiting the intrusion of slickens. The court did *not* ban hydraulic mining; it only blocked the run-off of materials into streams in the Mother Lode region. Almost all the mines soon found that the sole solution was construction of impoundment dams to prevent the flow of debris. In the 1880s such dams were not economically feasible, though some owners attempted to construct them.

In 1893, Anthony J. Caminetti, a U.S. congressman from Amador County in the Mother Lode sponsored the Caminetti Act creating an entity to be known as the California Debris Commission. The commission would be composed of three engineering officers from the U.S. Army, and it could grant licenses for hydraulic mines and could collect 3 percent of mining revenues for construction of dams. However, the commission never levied the tax because it would have brought only .45 cents per cubic yard of gravel processed, a figure so unrealistically low that it would not even justify the cost of collection much less dam construction.

The commission and some mining firms did build three concrete structures, known as training walls 85,100 feet long in the vicinity of Marysville to control discharge. These walls effectively confined millions of cubic yards of materials in the Yuba River that would have spilled into the Feather and Sacramento Rivers. However, this project primarily restrained materials previously disturbed by mining in an effort to avoid future suits against established mining concerns. The commission primarily helped clear blocked river channels to restore navigation, policed for clandestine operations, and supervised occasional efforts to restore mines which were willing to build localized restraining structures. The commission approved over 600 applications for renewal of hydraulic mining out of 1,000 proposed, yet few if any of the new permit holders followed through with effective debris dams. The Omega Mine, discussed below, was virtually the only exception.[4]

One other factor in ending hydraulic mining was the advent of technically more feasible methods of dredging in the 1890s. Dredging generated some slickens, though generally not as much as hydraulic mining since dredges processed and redeposited materials near the point of removal. Dredging removed topsoil but it left masses of gravel which were then accessible for road materials, concrete, etc. Dredges would eventually process much of the 6 million cubic yards of material left undeveloped at the time of the Sawyer Decision. However, some material could not be worked by dredges, so hydraulic mining remained economically viable if the cost of dam construction could be met.

The decline in hydraulic mining was not particularly important in the 1920s. Other forms of placer mining were also in the doldrums in that decade, as noted in chapter 2. However, the Pacific Gas and

Electric Co. did complete the Bullard's Bar Dam on the North Fork of the Yuba River in 1924, which allowed renewal of hydraulic mining behind the dam, but gold production was only a secondary consideration.

Even though hydraulic mining seemed destined to be relegated to the history books, some lobbying efforts continued over the years to find ways to provide loans for dams that could be paid off under the regulations of the Debris Commission. As early as 1925, the state legislature employed engineer Arthur Jarman to prepare a detailed report on potential dam sites and costs, but the legislature voted down any follow-up in 1927. In 1929 the legislature passed a bill which would have provided $200,000 for purchase of dam sites (but not outright construction) but Governor Young vetoed it.[5]

The general rise in the price of gold in the early 1930s brought new interest in hydraulic mining. In mid 1932, the Los Angeles Chamber of Commerce advanced a plan to restore hydraulic mining with the federal government providing loans to build dams under the Reconstruction Finance Corporation (R.F.C.). The Chamber of Commerce estimated that 50,000 workmen could be employed and considerable gold added to the overall money supply, but the real political focus for renewal of hydraulic mining still rested with the California Legislature.[6]

Final approval by the state legislature reflected a dramatic reversal in public opinion, and the mining community itself acknowledged that dam construction had to be sturdy and not "makeshift." In Marysville, California, the very community that had been the focus of the Sawyer Decision, various civic bodies passed resolutions favoring the building of dams on the Yuba River. W. T. Ellis, chair of the Yuba County Board of Supervisors, led the "valley interests" in questioning some details of the bill, though he made a statement supporting the basic principle of restoration of hydraulic mining if debris could be controlled. A. A. McMullen of the Anti-Debris Association expressed the same sentiments. Perhaps the most revealing incident occurred the next year when opposition arose to a permit for one development near Georgetown in the Mother Lode. The opponents actually dropped their complaint when the issue was aired at a public meeting. These views were shaped by the very real pressures of the Great Depression and the pressing need for any income that might be developed.[7]

The California Senate in 1933 unanimously passed the Placer District Act as Senate Bill 480, after the State House of Representatives passed it by a vote of 80 to 10. Attorney James D. Stewart, the author of the act, patterned it on various California irrigation laws which had provided water for agriculture using a district system. Stewart held large personal holdings of gold-bearing gravel on the North Fork of the American River (he had allowed about 100 people to work them with primitive methods), however, in spite of any self-interest, the bill had real merits. Walter W. Bradley called it splendid, and said that it had the potential of employing 50,000 workers.[8]

Under the act, mining firms in locations feasible for use of a common storage basin could unite into a Placer Mining District. Each district supplied water and constructed storage basins to impound the debris in coordination with the Army Corps of Engineers' Debris Commission. The act granted the districts the legal right of *eminent domain*, the power of mandatory purchase of property at a reasonable price, for sites for dam construction, ditches, and other works. The districts could issue bonds, which were legal investments for California savings banks. Though no mine owner could be forced to join a district, it was clearly to the owners' advantage to do so. In making district decisions, only the mine owners could vote.

Considerable activity anticipatory to complete restoration of hydraulicking was evident in the Mother Lode by the spring of 1934. Julia MacDonald, a prominent developer and mining broker at Placerville, California, was constructing "satisfactory impounding dams" of her own and already had one pump in operation. Just outside Oroville, California, the E. I. West Co. was developing 159 acres with a most unusual technique. The firm used a tower, cables and an 850 h.p. engine to move materials to a better location where the debris could be restrained.[9]

In 1934 federal legislation contributed to further renewal of hydraulic mining. California Rep. Harry Englebright sponsored an amendment to the Caminetti Act. By career, Englebright was himself a mining engineer and represented the congressional district that included most of the Mother Lode. The U.S. Congress passed the Englebright Amendment on June 19 with little debate or controversy, and under it the U.S. Army Corps of Engineers would control a fund to construct restraining works, settling reservoirs, etc.

The mining firms which actually removed gold-bearing materials would pay taxes for each cubic yard into a debris fund. At the outset the initial cost of dams had been a problem. Under the amendment the government could give advances to mine owners for construction of works to restrain debris. The R.F.C. and another New Deal agency, the Public Works Administration, administered the funds. This amendment drew little debate in Congress since the Silver Act was going through at the same time.[10]

By November 1934, the Eagle Rock District had already formed in one potential locale in California. The federal government initiated a $95,000 program to survey and prepare sites. Estimates of potential gold-bearing gravel available then ran as high as 500,000,000 cubic yards, which would mean as many as 3,000 workers could be employed. Oregon, too, allowed the use of powerful pumps in the placer areas in the southwest corner of that state, but these were in a much more confined locale than in California.[11]

Regarding hydraulicking equipment, the Joshua Hendry Iron Works of San Francisco and Sunnyvale, California, was the leader in producing the 1930s versions of the Little Giant pumps, as well as other equipment. Some demand had continued after the Sawyer Decision. A few operations had survived in California and some hydraulic mining had functioned at Idaho City, an old placer camp near Boise.[12] As late as 1932, estimates of remaining deposits there stood at 10 million cubic yards in a bank 90 feet deep. Four Little Giant pumps were recovering $.10 to $.22 per yard. Other major operations were ongoing in Alaska, British Columbia, and the Malay States (now called Malaysia). The U.S. military also used hydraulic equipment along the Panama Canal to remove landslide materials that created navigation hazards or blockages.[13]

By the spring of 1935, the California legislature further reflected the changed political climate regarding hydraulic mining (and mining in general) when it tabled a bill that would have required restoration of topsoil after dredging or hydraulic mining operations were completed. This issue also reflected deeper undercurrents resulting from a labor dispute. The dredging firms in Amador County in the Mother Lode had locked out the workers, and the labor organizations began the lobbying effort for soil restoration as a move to attack the companies. Later that year the legislature also defeated a proposed tax of 2–4 percent on placer gold production, to be collected on each 11 cubic feet. The argument prevailed that the small placer miner rather than the dredge or hydraulic operation would end up paying.[14]

In 1935, the U.S. Congress essentially finalized the "Giants' return." The Debris Commission, under the leadership of Col. T. H. Jackson, had studied potential dam sites, costs, etc., with the earlier Jarman Report in hand, and then issued its own report, which became known as the Jackson Report. A preliminary version of this report suggested four dam sites but essentially advised against using federal money to build them since returns to the government would be questionable.[15]

Mining interests attacked Jackson vehemently when the report appeared. James Stewart, the attorney behind California's approval of the Little Giants' return and owner of gold gravel himself, wrote a candid letter to Walter W. Bradley in early 1935. "Of all the asinine reasons for the government refusing to aid the hydraulic miner," he stated, "that of not having sufficient gold content has the longest ears of any jackass government report to date, which is sure going some."

He also noted that some parties, including himself, had illegally mined hydraulically after the Sawyer Decision, but the profits had led them to take the risk. It is remarkable that Stewart, a prominent attorney and political figure in California, would make such admissions in writing and to a high official. However, he knew Bradley well and knew he favored the renewal of hydraulic mining.[16]

Stewart was a powerful lobbyist and he and others asked for a hearing after the Jackson Report, at which they firmly maintained that the very purpose of the Caminetti Act had been federal control and coordination. Walter W. Bradley wrote a major article encouraging the project. The army revised the Jackson Report and placed a cost of $6.945 million on four possible dams, but suggested that the firms legally assure the government that they could operate for at least 20 years to repay the required loans. Congress then approved the project, but did not appropriate additional survey funds of $100,000 until 1936. Rep. Englebright sponsored the legislation and was not ashamed to take full credit for it in a letter to Bradley.[17]

In early 1938 the Debris Commission announced that the largest dam at Smartville would restrain materials on both the Middle and South Yuba Rivers. This dam, a gravity arch design 237 feet high, was obviously a major project in engineering and construction and would cost $4.595 million. It had considerable potential for power generation as well. Nearly 400,000,000 cubic yards of gold bearing gravel were present above this dam site. According to the Jackson Report, the material had a value averaging 18.2 cents per cubic yard and could be worked for 13.89 cents per cubic yard. With a projected annual production of 5.9 million cubic yards, the costs would be $819,000 with a net profit of $254,000.

Two other sites on the North and Middle forks of the American River called for concrete arch dams of 139 and 148 feet in height, which would allow development of 87 million and 76 million cubic yards respectively. The estimated costs were $825,000 and $800,000. Annual production could be about 1.3 and 1.2 million cubic yards. With values of 19.5 cents and 17.1 cents, the operators could expect to spend $175,000 and $158,000 to net $78,000 and $47,000, respectively. The fourth dam in the original proposal, on the Bear River, was ultimately canceled by litigation between mine owners and the Pacific Gas and Electric Co.[18]

The U.S. Army Corps of Engineers completed only two of the dams. The dam on the North Fork of the American River began operation in 1939 and the larger dam near Smartville, California, on the Yuba River commenced functioning in early 1941. This dam was first called the Narrows Dam but was later named for Harry Englebright, who had championed the project.[19]

The Corps of Engineers also began to prepare the site on the Middle Fork of the American River for what was supposed to be the Ruck-A-Chuky Dam. However, the army ordered the site changed after a landslide at the original site in mid 1940. A construction crew was preparing the alternate site just a month later when it discovered gold. The crew spent time, presumably in the evenings, working it themselves. A question immediately arose as to whether the government owned the vein or whether it was subject to mining claims. Finally, the army terminated the Ruck-A-Chuky Dam as well as the Bear River site. A dam to promote development of gold mines could not be built because it stood atop a gold mine![20]

By 1938, manufacturers of pumps were advertising extensively in mining journals for new customers expected from the restoration of hydraulic mining. Photographs of the new generations of the Little Giants looked much the same as equipment used in the prior century.[21]

The Klamath River and other sites in far northwest California were particularly active, especially around the town of Happy Camp, since there was no need to wait for dams. The Swanson Corp. used 25,000,000 gallons per day to run two Joshua Hendry Giants with four- and six-inch nozzles at its site in Trinity County. The Golden Eagle Co. purchased six Little Giant pumps and installed 3,000 feet of pipeline to supply them. Initially it employed six workers. Others which began or resumed operations in the area were the Curly Jack Mining Corp. and the Smith and Black hydraulic mine.[22]

By 1939 another mine was in operation behind the Bullards Bar Dam of the Pacific Gas and Electric Co. in addition to the one noted earlier. The Poverty Hill Mine was producing well by the placer season that year. The court had specifically enjoined this mine as part of the Sawyer Decision back in 1884, but new group bought the property in 1936 and wrote a contract with the Pacific Gas and Electric Co., which required an annual payment of $.02 per cubic yard for debris collected behind the dam. Unfortunately, some 100 feet of overburden sat atop the pay streak, so the site would produce a mass of debris but also good profit. In 1937, the firm conducted a series of tests and studied several possibilities for development, but decided to return to hydraulic mining instead. The next year, the firm installed Diesel pumps to supply water. When production began in 1939, the mine had a capacity of processing 30,000 cubic yards per hour. This increased to 100,000 cubic yards the next year with only a 40 percent increase in cost. The firm employed 33.[23]

Mining interests began responding to the renewed possibilities behind the major dams before they were completed. The owners of the Omega Mine, located above the Englebright Dam site, took special pleasure in the prospect of hydraulicking again since their property had been closed by the Sawyer Decision, but had later operated intermittently, only to be blocked by an injunction in 1931 when they tried to reopen with their own dam.[24]

Miners often applied for permits to remove water, a California state requirement. One firm applied for a permit allowing use of three cubic feet per second from the North Fork of the American River at a cost of $4,000. By 1940 some activity was ongoing on the North Fork of the American River, most notably at the Red Hill operation. The next year the opening of the Englebright Dam allowed several mines to resume operation after more than half a century.[25]

Unfortunately for the mine owners, World War II stopped hydraulic as well as lode production on almost all gold and silver mines. Hydraulic mining suffered the most since the war began just shortly after the new dams had come on-line. After the war, some recovery of gold mining in general was evident in early 1946. However, the overall economy soon developed an upward momentum that continued for several decades and with it a general return to prosperity. Quite simply, the Great Depression was over. As the director of the Bureau of Mines had summed up the pattern of the 1930s, "The time to mine gold is in hard times." The post-war period saw a return to prosperity making it emphatically not a time to mine gold.

The government's fixed price of $35 per ounce had worked to the benefit of the industry in 1934. The major burst of inflation in the late 1940s and early 1950s led to a period of rapidly rising labor, equipment, and energy costs. In this economic climate, the fixed gold price was a definite hinderance, and many lode gold mines, dredges, and placers could not sustain their profit margins for long after the end of World War II.

By 1957, only five hydraulic mines were operating behind the two major dams built to provide for them. Sixteen others still had valid licenses. By 1962, hydraulic mining had virtually ended but the placer mining districts had paid a total of $305,566 into a special fund and $302,524 had been returned to the federal government for construction of the dams and subsequent maintenance. This was far below the 1938 projections when the dams were in the planning stage. Considering the original cost of the dams at $4,646,872, hydraulic mines and mine owners had definitely received a benefit at public expense. When one considers the bad reputation the hydraulic method had and still has, this is even more ironic.

On the other hand, the Army Corps of Engineers and other federal agencies, like the Bureau of Reclamation, built many other dams which did not produce a return on costs from local activities such as irrigation and power generation. The two dams built for hydraulic mining were in appropriate sites and did provide flood control, recreation, etc. The Englebright Dam was equipped for power generation and returned its cost from that capacity alone.[26]

The Depression saw the return of a revived hydraulic mining industry, which had long been regarded as an environmentally destructive enterprise. In hindsight, it seems remarkable that this $100,000,000 industry had been shut down over $3,250,000 in damages, but one commentator summed up the situation by stating that this was a case of an "organized minority" outmanoeuvering an "unorganized majority." The technical progress available by the 1930s allowed "peace" between what had been disparate economic interests.

The conflict between farming and hydraulic mining in California represents a good example of a localized dispute between disparate but powerful economic interests. A similar situation provided the focus of what is now recognized as a classic study of Kansas at much the same time. Robert R. Dykstra in *The Cattle Towns* (1968) determined that two different commercial groups were present in five well-known "railhead" communities at the end of the famous trails from Texas. One group benefitted from the arrival of the Texans, who had driven their herds up the trails to be put on railroad cars. The other economic group depended on local trade with the farming economy. This latter group saw the influx of cattle as being destructive because herds often damaged farmlands and rowdy Texans often went on rampages in the towns. Ultimately, the settled community with a local base became dominant but only because the cattle trails themselves died.

Significantly, the farming community recognized that the situation had changed and that the increased economic activity would be of general value. Former opponents were willing to change their earlier position in one of the most remarkable political reversals ever. Robert L. Kelley, the author of *Gold vs. Grain*, a thorough study of hydraulic mining, noted the changed climate that allowed the return of hydraulic mining in the 1930s. However, he interpreted the alteration as being a result of agriculture, a small business, seeing mining as another small business. Also, in the interim, California, and especially the agricultural community, had a "war" with the "Octopus," the giant Southern Pacific Railroad, which made the earlier conflict over hydraulic mining seem minor.[27]

Estimates that as many as 50,000 workers could be employed in hydraulic mining were ludicrous. Even in the nineteenth century, the introduction of hydraulicking had the net effect of substantially reducing the man power involved in placering. Heavier equipment available in the 1930s meant that the larger hydraulic mines needed only a few dozen employees. Indeed, many areas that might have proved viable to hydraulic mining were accessible to dredging, a process that also required fewer employees.

As an interesting final observation, the authors of several academic histories of California discuss hydraulic mining in the nineteenth century, noting the damage to farming and the Sawyer Decision, but none mentioned the legal revival of the process in the 1930s.[28] It is true that the giant pumps which did return were not nearly as numerous as early projections had anticipated and were not as long-lasting. Even so, the return did represent an important principle: a changed political climate. The fact that the Little Giants returned so quietly, without a mass of publicity, is remarkable in itself.

Today some of the hydraulicked areas, disparaged as environmental disasters in earlier times, have been designated as state parks because they portray our heritage from the mining frontier days. Even in the 1930s, California retained a faith in mining as a solution to the imminent problems of the Great Depression. The Giants' return is just one more example of the significant frontier psychology that persisted long after the official end of that era of American development.

SEVEN

Aftermath

Two dramatic historic events clearly bracketed the Great Depression—the stock market crash of 1929 and the bombing of Pearl Harbor on December 7, 1941, twelve years later. During World War II the market for gold and silver fell, and these highly sought items in the Depression suddenly became materials of little consideration during a modern military conflict. The success of gold and silver mining in the 1930s made it possible to quickly revive copper, lead, and zinc mining for the war effort, and trained miners and equipment were readily diverted back to industrial metal recovery. The War Productions Board (W.P.B.) issued mandatory regulations allocating resources, and in 1942 the W.P.B. wrote Order L-208, which closed gold and silver mines producing more than 1,200 tons of ore per year, to make available skilled miners to produce the necessary industrial metals for the war effort. The U.S. Employment Service transferred miners to copper areas primarily in Arizona, Utah, and Montana. The order also effectively ended underground mining, dredge mining, and hydraulic mining solely for gold and silver. Subsequently Order P-5e addressed equipment, sending machinery to mines which produced industrial metals.[1]

After World War II, gold and silver mine owners successfully sued the government over Order L-208 and won a substantial settlement. In the interim, though, the miners themselves remained economically well-off. A few particular communities with economies based primarily on gold, like Cripple Creek, Colorado, and Lead, South Dakota, suffered, but even the Coeur d'Alene area, Leadville, Colorado, and other silver areas did well producing lead and other ancillary metals. Copper areas prospered.

There were complaints that manpower freed from gold and silver mines numbered only a few hundred. In reality virtually all these personnel went to industrial metals since workers in this field held critical occupations under military draft regulations (many volunteered for the armed services anyway). Some precious metal production continued from very small mines and as by-products from the mining of copper, lead, and zinc.

Considering mining only within the context of the period of the Great Depression, one is better able to evaluate the genuine significance of federal subsidies to gold and silver. Despite the contemporary media coverage of silver issues at the time, the first two decades of studies of the New Deal by insiders, opponents of it, and scholars failed to discuss the place of the silver issue. It was not until the 1950s that some scholarly analyses finally appeared.

The first major figure to express an opinion, a surprisingly negative one, was President Roosevelt's old rival, Herbert Hoover. Despite Hoover's background as a mining engineer and champion of the industry, he criticized the Silver Act in his 1952 memoirs because it only benefitted about 2,000 in the silver industry. He commented that the ratio for silver of 16 to 1 actually declined during President Roosevelt's tenure.[2]

Arthur M. Schlesinger, Jr., an advisor to the Kennedy administration and a prominent scholar of United States history, drew considerable notice during the early 1960s with publication of *The Coming of the New Deal*. In this book Schlesinger was the first to note Roosevelt's original opposition to the silver bill. He also discussed the cost of it, which he estimated at $1.5 billion (far more than farm price supports) and which he felt only benefitted 5,000 people in the silver industry. He also commented that the bill gave little impetus to inflation, even though the silver that the government purchased was used to back silver certificates issued by the U.S. Treasury. In summing up, he commented that the entire silver policy was the "most remarkable—and least remarked—special interest of the period."[3]

Another well-known historian, William Leuchtenburg, essentially echoed Schlesinger's opinion, but New Deal historian Frank Friedel concluded that silver purchases had, in fact, been mildly inflationary and noted that most silver was recovered as a by-product of copper mining.[4]

Nobel Prize Winner Milton Friedman has stated that the De-

Fig. 23—This cartoon in Pay Dirt, *a weekly mining news-
letter, from October 18, 1938, shows amazing foresight
about the future prospect of U.S. involvement in a war.*

pression was not the fault of Wall Street, big business, the excesses
of the 1920s, or the capitalist system. Friedman, the best-known
American spokesman for the monetarist school of thought, sees the
solution to economic problems in adjusting the supply of money in
circulation. He and other monetarists contend the Depression was
caused by mismanagement of the money supply in the crucial early
months after the Stock Market Crash of 1929. The crash could not

have been prevented; however, it definitely did not need to lead to an overall collapse if the Federal Reserve Board (F.R.B.) had not *further* contracted the money supply, thus transforming what could have been a relatively short crisis in the financial markets into a long-term disaster for the entire economy. A previous severe financial panic in 1907 lasted only a few months because the major banks had backed each other. In 1929, to use a metaphor from the field of medicine, the F.R.B. effectively bled a patient who desperately needed a transfusion.

Congress presumably established the Federal Reserve Board as an official agency to help adjust the supply of money in circulation to compensate for variations in the economy. Had the F.R.B. acted appropriately and simply increased the overall money supply in 1929, some individuals and investment firms would have suffered severe losses, but the situation would have soon improved with adequate money moving throughout the economy.

Regarding subsidies, Friedman stated that silver cost the government $5 for every $1 of aid to the mining industry.[5] Critics who point out that Roosevelt initially opposed the silver bill invariably gloss over the fact that the president did in fact sign the bill and gave Secretary Morgenthau instructions to be "enthusiastic" in enforcing the new law.[6] There is little doubt that a Roosevelt veto would have been overridden by the House but not the Senate. Further, Roosevelt himself had espoused silver in the 1932 campaign and issued a 1933 executive order giving higher prices long *before* the final Silver Act. Always the master politician, he seemed to be playing this issue at some distance; if it failed he could drop it but could claim success if it worked to any noticeable extent. When Congress seemed sure to enact the Silver Act, he sent a favorable message to that body which specifically requested the measure.[7]

Schlesinger's criticism that the cost of the Silver Act, $1.5 billion over the subsequent 15 years, was a sum far more than farm price supports but for only "5,000 people in the silver industry," overlooks the fact that silver purchases were in the form of a straight subsidy, which resulted in stockpiling a valuable material that could be stored indefinitely. Agricultural price supports, on the other hand, gave taxpayers' money to farmers to *not* grow hogs, cotton, wheat, etc. At least three leading newspapers in mining locales, the *Arizona Republic*, the *Coeur d'Alene Press*, and the *Sacramento Union*, noted some potential "loopholes" at the time of the bill's passage, but the law did provide for a goal of one-quarter of the total precious metal reserve, even though it did not place any limits on when silver had to rise to that level.[8] Consequently, the executive branch could have administratively minimized the cost of the Silver Act, but chose not to do so. As early as December 1933, some months before the final act passed, President Roosevelt had already ordered a significant price rise to 64.64 cents per ounce. On April 24, 1935, he ordered a new price of 77.57 cents per ounce. Obviously, he could have avoided the additional cost by just leaving the fixed price at 64.64 cents, and, indeed, he lowered the price back to 64.64 cents on December 31, 1937, since the genuine market price was falling. He could have issued even lower prices over the next several years.

Regarding Schlesinger's statement that the Silver Act cost $1.5 billion, this figure is excessive. The government would undoubtedly have purchased a major volume of silver with or without a subsidy, and the $1.5 billion cited would have covered silver subsidies through the 1940s. As can be seen in the figures in the Appendix, Table A.1, from 1934 through 1942 the annual *difference* between the subsidized price of silver paid by the government and foreign prices amounted to $331,391,655. True, the higher number cited by Schlesinger was for a longer period, but the effective end of purchases noted in 1943–44 (the result of L-208) could have served as a precedent for adjustments after the war.

Schlesinger's figure of 5,000 people who benefitted refers only to those in mines that were primarily silver producers. Within just two weeks of the bill's passage, Phelps Dodge Corporation and Miami Copper Corporation, two major Arizona firms, announced that they would reemploy a total of 1,000 miners. The companies specifically gave the silver bill the credit because silver is an important by-product of many copper ores. Others soon followed.[9] Milton Friedman and Frank Friedel noted this aspect but Schlesinger and others overlooked it. Finally, Schlesinger's claim that the bill gave little impetus to inflation is belied by the introduction of new silver certificates into the money supply. See the Appendix for a detailed discussion of the complex interrelationships between inflation, government policy, and the role of silver and gold during the Great Depression.

There were other effects that carried forward from Depression-era mining, particularly in land and resource policies. The Taylor Grazing Act, passed in 1934, gave Roosevelt the legal authority to end the Homestead Act of 1862 regarding occupancy of farmsteads (which gave the possibility to parties living on open government lands to be given the land for free after five years), and he subsequently issued an executive order to this effect. However, the Taylor Grazing Act specifically and explicitly continued the Mining Law of 1872, and this law was an integral part of the automobile gold rush and renewed interest in silver. Several factors contributed to the Mining Law being retained, to the disgust of many in the environmental movement in recent years.

At the time of the Depression there was little understanding of nature's ability to rehabilitate itself or the consequences of long-term environmental damage, and a different national consciousness regarding unlimited resources and man's right to dominate and subjugate nature prevailed. Moreover, finding meaningful employment was a dominant public attitude during this era, and issues regarding environmental damage from the use of particular methods were not considered of primary importance. Hydraulic mining epitomized the environmental damage that could occur, but negligent attitudes pervaded the use of almost all mining processes. Mining firms abandoned depleted properties leaving open shafts, potential groundwater pollution, and other long-term problems. Only since the 1970s have federal laws and regulations become more stringent. Recently the present writer helped survey the town of Midvale, Utah, as part of a Superfund clean up of the USSR & M smelter, the same smelter discussed in chapter 5.

The USSR & M smelter had operated from the turn of the century into 1970. The proportion of tailings left there during the 1930s was relatively minor in the overall cleanup process, and, as at many other sites, development had occurred at mines and mills which had long histories of production prior to Depression-era mining. Even in the 1950s, the uranium rush saw unregulated mining and milling activities which resulted in intense cleanup efforts in more recent years. Also the massive increases in mining in World War II and subsequent open-pit copper mining occurred at a level that dwarfed activities in the 1930s.

During mineral development of the 1930s the country still looked to the West, with its largely undeveloped and seemingly limitless resources, for the ultimate solution to many national problems. As mentioned in the Introduction this attitude is associated with the nineteenth-century values and was manifest in the school of academic thought put forth by historian Frederick Jackson Turner in 1893. Turner, as well as the U.S. Bureau of the Census, had proclaimed the physical frontier essentially at an end by 1890. During that same decade a massive political movement for "free silver" gave living testament to a widespread popular belief that the frontier was *not* dead but that the western United States still possessed the resources to end economic hard times, both for the little man and the larger mining/industrial complex. It was fanned by a belief in the viability of new discoveries that extended through the 1930s and after and was associated with concepts such as individualism and self-reliance, attitudes carried forward from the nineteenth century and which recurred during the 1930s whenever the topic of mining arose. Frontier concepts were also manifest in the activities of people who turned toward mining to make whatever livelihood that they could and avoid the dole. Virtually every reporter, researcher, and official who mentioned the topic at all made similar observations about the relationship of 1930s mining to the earlier frontier period.

In one of the most controversial points of his thesis, Turner also theorized that the frontier provided a "safety valve" as an outlet for large numbers of the unemployed workers in eastern cities especially during times of economic troubles. Turner's critics have observed that those who moved to the frontier were rarely from urban backgrounds but were instead from settled rural areas. Further, the times of greatest migration can be easily documented to have also been times of economic prosperity.[10]

However, the 1930s automobile gold rush manifests many aspects of Turner's views in terms of providing a true social "safety valve." It was indeed a time of the economic stress and many people from more populous regions did go to relatively unpopulated areas and disbursed over the large western region. Some came directly from major cities, others of rural origin were diverted from migration to cities by the appeal of gold recovery in placer areas. Overall, the pattern suggested by Turner seems quite valid, especially within California where, as noted in chapter 2, a tenth of the population attempted placering at some time in the early 1930s.

Even in the Great Depression, the American people showed that they still adhered to the psychology Turner attributed to a frontier experience. Certainly a wide range of reporters, editorialists, and even bureaucrats could not resist the colorful image of the mining frontier returning to help rescue the nation from one of the greatest crises it had faced. Of all the contemporary sources that are available for study of the period, the one that most emphasized the frontier theme as returned to the present was the *Idaho Daily Statesman*. Though a staid, very conservative organ in its political outlook, the *Statesman* actively promoted mining and its relationship to mining history in feature articles almost every Sunday with many other articles on weekdays. Perhaps this paper summarized the entire movement the best of any source at the end of the placer season of 1932. It published a poem by Clarence Eddy—a man described as an Idaho Poet Prospector—which was dedicated to both historical and current mining.

> And they are bold who woo the gold,
> For some win but a grave,
> But they win best who love the quest,
> Nor court her as a slave,
> And well they woo who dare and do,
> For fortune loves the brave.[11]

Clearly the romance of the frontier and the psychological manifestations of frontier thinking survived long after the physical frontier had closed in the belief that the western U.S. would somehow provide a solution to all problems, personal or national. Many demonstrated that they believed the frontier of the 1930s would provide personal and national solutions to the severe economic problems the country faced, and demonstrated this by prospecting and mining on both an individual basis and as entrepreneurs in a wide range of commercial mining operations. At the highest official levels, the same factors promoted mining policies for both gold and silver as monetary sources which, those officials believed, could end the national Depression.

Appendix

The entire topic of inflation, government policy, and the roles of gold and silver prior to and during the Great Depression entails a more detailed inspection of the entire monetary situation in the 1930s.

Though many politicians and scholars have portrayed Herbert Hoover as the "villain" in bringing about the Depression, the initial source of mismanagement came from the F.R.B., as noted in chapter 7. Hoover took some potent remedial actions. In 1932, when the economy was particularly desperate, he took $750 million in gold from the government deposits and placed it in circulation in coinage and in issues of new Federal Reserve Notes. The economy responded, as monetary theory stated it would ($P=M/T$), and Hoover's R.F.C. functioned to distribute the increased money placed in circulation.[1] Unfortunately for Hoover, these actions were not enough to affect the next election.

It is ironic that one of Roosevelt's first actions was the removal of gold as circulating currency. Under the President's Executive Orders it became illegal to possess more than $100 in gold coin, bullion, or gold certificates (aside from rare coin and art objects). Banks and individuals surrendered gold and gold certificates, thus driving currency, including that recently released by Hoover, out of circulation. Many individuals illegally held on to some gold, but this portion was also driven out of circulation and went literally "underground." The Treasury's official reports noted that $287 million in gold was still outstanding in 1934, but records for circulation of gold were dropped from Treasury reports that year. Small amounts drifted into the Treasury in subsequent years, but the bulk was of no economic value until Roosevelt's Executive Orders were relaxed in 1954.[2]

Roosevelt maintained a major supply of gold as currency backing, but holders of paper notes could no longer exchange them for actual gold.[3] In addition to gold bullion and coins, which had circulated in the financial community (though rarely with the general public), the nation also lost the use of gold certificates, which had been an important part of the overall supply of circulating currency. However, the Treasury could print more Federal Reserve Notes, theoretically backed by the gold, even though the notes themselves could no longer be directly exchanged for it. In essence, the bulk of the circulating money supply became paper, unbacked by gold or silver. Unbacked paper money is called fiat money. The Federal Reserve Board, not the Treasury, technically controls the bulk of notes placed in circulation. However, an administration can indirectly influence Federal Reserve Board activities since it appoints the membership for rotating terms. In essence, practical control of the money supply shifted from the F.R.B. to the Treasury under Roosevelt and the Banking Act of 1935 restructured the Federal Reserve System.

After 1933, the only exceptions to fiat money were silver certificates and silver coins. Roosevelt also "nationalized" silver, but with a crucial difference—the public could still hold and circulate silver coins and certificates, and the government held enough bullion and silver dollars to *redeem* all outstanding silver certificates. Private possession of silver bullion was illegal; holders had to surrender it at $.5001 per ounce. Silver art objects were still allowed. The net result, then, was somewhat different from the gold policy.

The government *could* have bought silver at the prevailing international market prices listed in Table A.1. Instead it paid extra because of the silver purchase measures passed by Congress in 1933 and 1934 (the Silver Purchase Act). The subsidy price, also shown in Table A.1, was completely the choice of President Franklin D. Roosevelt, and the president designated silver as worth $1.29 per ounce in backing silver certificates. The difference between the subsidized prices of 64.64 cents, 71.11 cents, and 77.57 cents, and the value for currency backing was attributed to "seignorage" (the cost of minting). Yet relatively little of the silver took the form of coins; the great bulk simply went to the West Point Depository as bullion. (Ironically, silver for jewelry, tableware, etc., came from foreign sources on the open market during this period since domestic producers were better off selling to the Treasury. However, the U.S. did purchase both gold and silver from foreign sources.)[4]

In 1933 the Treasury had no silver stock in bullion at all, though the government did hold over $500 million in silver dollars. The stock of bullion rose dramatically with the purchase program, reaching $1.037 billion by mid 1938. At that time the government still

Table A.1. Silver Purchases, 1934–1944

Year	Govt. Price	Market Price	Annual Purchase at Subsidy Price	Difference in Actual Purchase Price from Market Price
1934	$.6464	$.4254	$ 5,531,995	$ 1,891,354
1935	.6464°	.5764	155,587,533	21,305,040
1936	.7757	.5534	256,540,620	102,177,370
1937	.7757	.4530	77,453,735	32,221,633
1938	.7757°°	.4454	151,082,730	56,451,532
1939	.6464	.4300	153,023,320	51,238,200
1940	.7111	.3548	78,207,206	39,186,183
1941	.7111	.3506	31,949,309	16,197,060
1942	.7111	.3529	21,282,147	10,721,283
1943	.7111	.4346	5,141	2,000
1944	No Purchase			
Totals:			930,663,736	331,391,658

SOURCE: U.S. Dept. of the Treasury, *Annual Report, Secretary of the Treasury* (Washington: Government Printing Office), year 1934, pp. 119–20, year 1935, pp. 135–36, year 1936, pp. 165–67, year 1937, pp. 171–72, year 1938, pp. 184–85, year 1939, pp. 173–74, year 1940, pp. 366–67, year 1941, pp. 254–55, year 1942, pp. 184–85, year 1943, pp. 264–65, year 1944, pp. 245–56.

°FY 1935 (July 1, 1934, to June 30, 1935) price was $.6464 until April 10; $.7111 until April 24; and $.7757 through the rest of that FY.

°°FY 1938 price was $.7757 to Dec. 31, 1937 and then $.6464.

held a stock of over 500 million silver dollars, not counting 39 million in circulation. The silver stock, bullion, and dollars backed $1.230 billion in circulating silver certificates plus a little over $1 million in older Treasury Notes of 1890 which were still outstanding but in a recall process.

Roosevelt's gold policy contrasted with silver on some important

Table A.2. Gold Acquisitions*

Fiscal Year	Actual Value	Equivalent Total Cost at Old Price	Difference
1932	$413,057,073	. . .	. . .
1933*	465,109,665	. . .	. . .
1934**	989,932,127	$619,532,000	$370,400,127
1935	1,301,432,721	768,588,950	532,843,771
1936	1,451,011,081	856,925,690	595,086,391
1937	1,762,927,433	1,041,134,500	721,792,933
1938	1,129,033,865	666,775,150	463,258,715
1939	3,224,890,528	1,904,528,100	1,320,362,428
1940	3,085,599,169	1,822,266,700	1,263,332,469
1941	3,529,187,190	2,084,237,100	1,444,950,090
1942	664,440,587	392,399,610	272,040,977
1943	188,134,966	111,107,130	77,027,836
1944	58,524,201	34,562,720	23,961,481

SOURCE: U.S. Dept. of the Treasury, *Annual Report, Secretary of the Treasury* (Washington: Government Printing Office), year 1932, pp. 177–78, year 1933, pp. 121–22, year 1934, pp. 119–20, year 1935, pp. 135–36, year 1936, pp. 165–67, year 1937, pp. 171–72, year 1938, pp. 184–85, year 1939, pp. 173–74, year 1940, pp. 366–67, year 1941, pp. 254–55, year 1942, pp. 184–85, year 1943, pp. 264–65, year 1944, pp. 245–56.

*The official gold price was $20.67 per ounce prior to April 8, 1933. During the period from Oct. 1933, to Jan. 31, 1934, President Roosevelt daily adjusted the price. The final, "permanent" price of $35 came one day after an Act of Congress allowed that adjustment.

**The 1934 total included $26,114,858 purchased at $20.67, $800,047,115 at $35, and the remainder at a range of prices.

points. Beginning in the fall of 1933, he adjusted the price paid for gold from $20.67 per ounce to reach a final price of $35.00 per ounce on January 31, 1934. This, in effect, produced a subsidy for the mining industry as did the Silver Act. The purchase price was also the value designated for currency backing, even though currency could not actually be exchanged for gold. Even at the $20.67 per ounce payment rate, gold was highly sought. As shown in Table A.2, the Treasury purchased nearly 20 million ounces at this price in 1932, and over 22.5 million ounces in 1933. With the change in prices in 1934, that year does not provide a good comparative time frame, and even Milton Friedman's highly sophisticated analyses stress the lack of definite figures for the period. However, 1935, the first full year of the price of $35 per ounce, saw purchases jump to over 37 million ounces. By 1941 total acquisitions were over 100 million ounces, though it must be pointed out the later years also had very high figures because gold was flowing into the United States from European countries and many private parties transferred wealth to the United States because of the rise of Nazism. When war broke out in 1939, governments purchased masses of American goods. These processes resulted in increases of U.S. gold stocks. Even with these considerations, however, most of the total increase in gold was due to purchases from mines.

Comparison of Table A.1 with Table A.2 shows the massive difference in the subsidy paid for silver, year by year, compared to gold. Yet gold has not received overall negative evaluations by historians and economists. Friedman stated that FDR's initial gold policy did achieve some inflation and aided prices of United States commodities by increasing foreign demand.[5]

In short, a gold policy congruous with the silver policy would have designated a still higher value for gold than the purchase price for currency backing. True, the price jump plus purchases did help to increase the government's holdings from $4.317 billion on June 30, 1933, to $7.856 billion on June 30, 1934. At this date virtually all of the increase was from internal events in the United States rather than European sources. The increase caused the nation's overall stock of money available to increase from $10.078 billion to $13.634 billion. Yet the total money in circulation actually *fell* from $5.72 billion to $5.37 billion, because the Treasury was calling in gold coin and gold certificates but was not adding paper currency.

It is remarkable that inflation did occur at all in this period, but the psychological climate can certainly be credited along with resolution of the banking crisis. The Federal Deposit Insurance Corporation (F.D.I.C.) restored public confidence in the banking system so currency that had been hidden in mattresses flowed back into the economy. The F.D.I.C. was not a Roosevelt proposal but was entirely a Congressional program from the first days of the New Deal.[6]

Tables A.3 and A.4 summarize the overall money supply and gold holdings. In subsequent years the circulating money supply did in-

Table A.3. Money Stocks (in Millions)

Fiscal Year	Gold Bullion	Silver Bullion	Silver Dollars	% of Gold to Total Money*	% of Gold to Circul. Paper $*	Gold Price Per Oz.
1929	4,109	. . .	540	50.64	115.84	$20.67
1930	4,535	. . .	540	54.59	135.82	20.67
1931	4,956	. . .	540	54.58	135.59	20.67
1932	3,919	. . .	540	43.52	96.19	20.67
1933	4,318	. . .	540	42.84	93.04	**35.00
1934	7,856	1.6	540	57.62	172.96	35.00
1935	9,115	313	546	60.32	206.69	35.00
1936	10,608	708	547	60.96	221.04	35.00
1937	12,318	835	547	63.57	267.55	35.00
1938	12,963	1,037	547	64.50	275.69	35.00
1939	16,110	1,231	547	67.82	320.02	35.00
1940	19,963	1,353	547	70.15	352.39	35.00
1941	22,624	1,436	547	69.03	313.49	35.00
1942	22,737	1,506	547	63.44	230.97	35.00
1943	22,388	1,520	539	54.78	150.84	35.00
1944	21,173	1,520	494	47.26	106.67	35.00

SOURCE: U.S. Dept. of the Treasury, *Annual Report, Secretary of the Treasury, 1944* (Washington: Government Printing Office, 1945), pp. 776–77 (summary tables for years 1913–44).

*The percent of gold to total money was officially released in the Annual Reports of the Treasury. However, the category listed next, percent of gold to circulating currency (backed by gold, not silver), is even more revealing.
**See text.

crease in some measure with new issues of Federal Reserve Notes, backed by gold. However, many of the new notes served only to offset retirement of other older forms of paper currency, specifically National Bank Notes. From 1935 to 1936, for example, Federal Reserve Notes in circulation increased $779 million, from $3.223 billion to $4.002 billion, but about half of this increase was canceled by retirement of other forms of paper currency. The paper retired was $391 million, leaving the actual increase in gold backed paper currency at $387 million.

The increase in the *total* supply of circulating currency jumped from $5.567 billion to $6.241 billion. Some $253 million more in silver certificates plus $23 million more in silver coinage made up the difference. In terms of increase in the money supply, silver was very important, almost as important as the increase allowed with a far

Table A.4. Circulating Currency

Year	Fed. Res. Notes	Other Paper Gold Backed	Gold Coin	Silver Certif.	Total (incl. coins, etc.)
1929	1,693	1,854	368	387	4,746
1930	1,402	1,937	357	387	4,522
1931	1,708	1,947	363	377	4,822
1932	2,780	1,709	452	353	5,695
1933	3,061	1,580	321	361	5,721
1934	3,068	1,474	...	401	5,373
1935	3,223	1,187	...	701	5,567
1936	4,002	797	...	955	6,241
1937	4,169	676	...	1,078	6,447
1938	4,114	588	...	1,230	6,461
1939	4,484	550	...	1,454	7,047
1940	5,163	502	...	1,582	7,848
1941	6,684	533	...	1,714	9,612
1942	9,310	534	...	1,754	12,383
1943	13,747	1,095	...	1,649	17,421
1944	18,750	1,099	...	1,588	22,504

SOURCE: U.S. Dept. of the Treasury, *Annual Report, Secretary of the Treasury, 1944* (Washington: Government Printing Office, 1945), pp. 776–77 (summary tables for years 1913–44).

larger stock of gold. It is quite significant to note that this period from June 30, 1935, to June 30, 1936, was one of further recovery in the overall economy.

By comparison, the period from June 30, 1937, to June 30, 1938, was one of a marked downturn, which Roosevelt's political opponents attributed to him, calling it the "Roosevelt Recession." In fact, the circulating quantity of Federal Reserve Notes fell during this period, from $4.169 billion to $4.114. Older paper currency also fell. The only categories which the Treasury increased were silver certificates and coins. Hence silver based currencies *alone* offset the fall in paper money, indeed it surpassed that loss to increase the entire circulating money supply marginally from $6.447 billion to $6.461 billion.

Without silver, the downturn that began in late 1937 would obviously have been even worse. An additional revealing fact is the proportion of gold to the total money stock (all money available, either circulating or held by the government). With the additional gold acquired by the government as the 1930s progressed, the ratio of gold on deposit to the total stock rose from 57.62 percent in 1934 (after the new price) to 64.50 percent in 1938. By comparison, the ratio was only 50 to 52 percent in the later 1920s, and it had been as low as 35 percent in 1920. Even more remarkable was the ratio of gold to paper currency actually circulating, which was backed by it (whether or not the currency could in fact be exchanged). Figures in the far column of the first section of Tables A.3 and A.4 show conclusively that the proportion of gold increased dramatically since the government was buying much more than required for currency backing. The increase from 207 percent to 352 percent from 1935 to 1941 was massive. Significantly, federal law only required a 40 percent stock for backing.

In short, the government was capable of using gold to back a *much* larger proportion of paper money than it did in the 1930s while still maintaining enough gold to assure confidence in the currency in the financial community and with the public. Further, the capability to use gold to back paper money grew markedly through the troubled decade of the 1930s. This capability was quite evident to the government even within the context of the 1930s and prior history. The example of inflation from increased money supply is obvious even without the conditions evident in World War II or later years, which saw full removal of gold as currency backing. Even a policy of automatically issuing new currency while keeping the ratio at approximately that of 1935 would certainly have avoided the downturn of 1937 and ended the Depression within another year.

Some inflation would have ultimately resulted but introduction of new money over months or years would have minimized this side-effect. In hindsight, it seems ludicrous that the government put so much into gold, which could have backed more new currency, yet the old joke about "gold bricks" was literally true. Gold served no useful purpose; much of it did not even serve as intended currency backing, and the government was acquiring so much from the imbalance in trade and investments by the later 1930s that it could have ended direct purchases and still raised the money stock.

Why was the government so stingy in printing more money? Franklin D. Roosevelt himself evaluated the example of the German Weimar Republic of the 1920s, which had seen a devastating inflation of hundreds of percent *a day*. Workmen were paid three times per day because the money had lost its value within hours; shoppers arrived at stores with wheelbarrows full of paper currency just to buy a loaf of bread.[7] Germany's situation had been appalling but it bore no resemblance to the United States.

Gradual increases in the money supply could have kept inflation under control and eased the lack of currency sufficiently to provide real relief. The fact that the nation had growing gold deposits yet utilized them so marginally was an outright tragedy. Overall, silver accomplished far more than scholars have been willing to admit. Meanwhile, gold received a *much greater* subsidy from the government while giving relatively little aid to the economy. However, the American mining industry and the Western United States in general profited from both policies, despite government purchases of some foreign gold and silver.

Friedman and Friedel, though of opposing economic opinions in other areas, briefly observed the modest inflation that did occur and its relation to the increase in the money supply. Yet neither of them, nor other commentators, criticized other monetary policies based on gold that provided much larger subsidies to mining. In 1941 alone the difference between $20.67 and $35.00 meant almost $1.5 billion more in government purchase costs. A system adjusted year by year, as was done with silver, would have saved money while still providing the same volume of gold. For a period prior to the final price rise to \$35 per ounce, Roosevelt ordered daily purchases above the old price at whatever he jokingly felt like that day.[8] Compared to the final figure of \$35, the silver subsidies listed in Table A.1 were trivial.

In addition to the modest inflation which resulted from silver, the policy should also receive credit for helping to establish confidence in the New Deal's monetary system. Roosevelt's Executive Orders were quite controversial, and the fact that currency could no longer be exchanged for gold could have had disastrous consequences had the New Deal not been able to establish considerable psychological confidence that the economy was improving.

The presence of silver certificates which still circulated provided a psychological incentive the other way. A succinct statement of Gresham's Law is, "Bad money drives out good." If two forms of currency are legally circulating, the public will use the one perceived to be of less value and hoard the other. When new forms of currency are introduced, the older currency is usually perceived as more valuable and is soon lost as a circulating medium. In essence, paper money backed by any specie is good money; unbacked paper money is bad money. Another excellent example from the 1960s involved coins. The advent of "clad" dimes, quarters, and half dollars soon drove all older coins of these denominations out of circulation since the older coins had some genuine silver content.

However, the 1930s silver policy proved a rare exception to the overall principle of Gresham's Law. The average person knew that he or she could still receive silver, a material of value on its own, in exchange for paper money designated as silver certificates. True, silver certificates were in the small denominations—one and five dollar bills—but these were more likely to be noticed and circulated most frequently, and many ordinary people felt comfortable with the notion that they could exchange Federal Reserve Notes for Silver Certificates, then exchange the certificates for actual silver if they needed to. The fact that the total of silver certificates was not nearly equal to Federal Reserve Notes in face value was not readily apparent. Yet the psychological value of Silver Certificates cannot be overemphasized, especially considering the fact that Federal Reserve Notes were already fiat money for all practical purposes.

The Silver Certificates, still exchangeable for precious metal, were the "good" money. Yet the small denominations forced them to circulate anyway while providing a psychological bridge to acceptance of more Federal Reserve Notes.

Even though it is obvious that World War II ended the Depression, the economics of why the war had this effect are often overlooked. The government simply issued more currency despite a large but now static supply of gold and silver. Even by 1944, as shown in Tables A.3 and A.4, there was still more gold than the face value of the circulating paper money backed by it. Inflation ultimately did result, though delayed until after the war by price controls as well as purchases of government savings bonds. Had the increase in paper money occurred evenly in a peace-time economy, inflation would not have been as marked as it was during the immediate post-war period. However, those who suffered through the Depression and who later saw the sharp inflation of 1946–49 found the latter preferable.

Taking a longer historical view, the subsidies to silver and gold were certainly important—perhaps crucial—to the Allied victory in World War II. A healthy overall mining industry readily abandoned precious metals to recover copper, lead, and zinc, vital for the war effort. Friedel and Friedman noted the aid to copper but failed to acknowledge the previous subsidization of precious metals and their contribution to the war effort.

Why was the subsidy crucial? Even the old price of $20.67 stimulated considerable gold production which would have continued. However, the escalation in mining effort after the rise to $35.00 an ounce certainly resulted in large part from the price being fixed at the higher level. Silver was even more dramatic in its increase with the subsidy.

Though copper was the most important ore during World War II, silver also had military applications, and some silver was needed by the Allies under the Lend-Lease program. Supplies were forthcoming from the West Point Depository.

The primary value of subsidies was the contribution they made to the overall health of the mining industry. Mining is a business that is extremely sensitive to relatively small price fluctuations. The bottom line is that market price changes of only a few cents can bring mines back into operation or drive them out of operation. To assume that subsidies of $1 to the industry at a cost to the government of $5 without considering ancillary benefits is misleading since the overall benefits of subsidies was much greater.

The money that the industry received for gold and silver did not simply disappear into the pockets of the mine owners. Much of the profits went for purchases of new equipment from manufacturers across the United States. The success of these firms in the 1930s meant that they could adjust and key up production to meet needs of the wartime effort in the 1940s.

The psychological need to maintain certain levels of gold in Fort Knox, even in the face of shortages of circulating currency and the need to accumulate more gold from mining and from the international balance of trade were very real aspects of the times. So was the psychological need for currency that was backed with sufficient gold and silver. Ultimately the concept of the necessity of currency backing withered away as the public became accustomed to the idea.

Abbreviations

AR *Arizona Republic*, Phoenix

BL [Walter W.] Bradley Papers, Bancroft Library, University of California, Berkeley

CC *Times Record*, Cripple Creek, Colo.

CdA *Coeur d'Alene Press*, Coeur d'Alene, Idaho

COSH Colorado State Historical Society, Denver, Colo.

DP *Denver Post*

E&MJ *Engineering and Mining Journal*

HDI *Helena Daily Independent*, Helena, Mont.

IDS *Idaho Daily Statesman*, Boise

LHD *Herald Democrat*, Leadville, Colo.

MD *Mountain Democrat*, Placerville, Calif.

NYT *New York Times*

PC *Prescott Evening Courier*, Arizona

RMN *Rocky Mountain News*, Denver, Colo.

SB *Sacramento Bee*

SU *Sacramento Union*

TE *Tombstone Epitaph*, Arizona

YMS *Yuma Morning Sun*, Arizona

Notes

Chapter 1—Beginnings

1. The Mother Lode region in California drew the original gold rush of 1848–49. It consists of nine counties (Amador, Placer, El Dorado, Nevada, Sierra, Mariposa, Madera, Tuolumne, and the most famous, Calaveras) as well as adjacent areas of four more counties.

2. "Autos Speed to New Mines," *San Francisco Examiner*, Dec. 18, 1930.

3. H. Bret Helendy and Benjamin Gilbert, *The Governors of California* (Georgetown, Calif.: Talisman Press, 1965), pp. 362–67.

4. "Gov. Rolph Asks Cooperation of State Legislature," SU, Jan. 7, 1931.

5. "New Gold Rush to California Held on Way," *Press Democrat*, Santa Rosa, Calif., Mar. 1, 1931.

6. "Men and Money Make Mines, Even Gold Mines," E&MJ 132, no. 2, p. 49.

7. Walter W. Bradley, "An Echo of the Days of '49," E&MJ 135, no. 11, pp. 494–96; L. H. Robbins, "'Off Gold': The Nations Still Feverishly Seek the Metal," NYT, May 28, 1933; "They're Not Getting Rich in New Gold Rush, But It's Lots of Fun," *Los Angeles Times*, Mar. 4, 1931.

8. "Jobless Workingmen Pan Gold Along Park's Bar," SB, April 28, 1931.

9. "Activity in Mines Gains," MD, July 22, 1931; "Hangtown Yields

Nuggets Valued at $25," MD, May 23, 1931; "Prospector Pans Dollar Dated 1795," SB, May 19, 1931.

10. B. H. Vandeveer, ed., *Who's Who in California* (Los Angeles: Who's Who Publ., 1940), pp. 86–87.

11. Letter, June 6, 1931, from Burley Tucker to Walter W. Bradley in carton 3, folder 1931, BL.

12. Bradley, "An Echo of the Days of '49," E&MJ 135, no. 11, p. 49.

13. "Increasing Gold Prospecting Embraces Entire World," E&MJ 132, no. 4, p. 182; "Rich Strike in Utah Leads to Gold Rush," CC, Aug. 12, 1931; "Prospector Finds Virgin Placer Bed," LHD, July 14, 1931.

14. "California Jobless Seek Gold in Hills," NYT, Oct. 11, 1931.

15. U.S. Dept. of Commerce, Bureau of the Census, of the U.S.: 1940, Population, vol. 1 (Washington: Government Printing Office, p. 130 (includes historic as well as 1940 statistics); "Twin Sisters Locate Twin Gold Mines," and "Long Toms Are Back in Use Along Deer Creek," SB, May 10, 1932; "Urge to Pan for Gold Brings Rush at Library," SB, June 21, 1932; "State Witnesses Gold Rush," SU, May 2, 1932; "Placer Mining to Be Resumed Near Site of Discovery," SU, May 22, 1932.

16. Bradley, "An Echo of the Days of '49," E&MJ 135, no. 11, p. 49; "Girl Gold Miners Got Small Yields," NYT, Feb. 22, 1933; State of Arizona, Bureau of Geology and Mineral Technology [Eldred D. Wilson], "Gold Placers and Placering in Arizona," Bulletin 168, (Tucson: University of Arizona, 1961, 3d ed.; 1st ed.,1933); Idaho Bureau of Mines and Geology [W. W. Staley], "Elementary Methods of Placer Mining," Pamphlet #35, Moscow: University of Idaho, 1931; New Mexico School of Mines [E. H. Wells and T. P. Wootton], "Gold Mining and Gold Deposits in New Mexico" (Socorro: N.M. School of Mines, 1932), pp. 3–6; "Scores Seeking Information on Gold Mines," YMS, April 26, 1932; "Amateur Gold Rush Reported in California," YMS, May 11, 1932; "Success of Placer Mines School Brings Demand from Other Cities," HDI, Aug. 7, 1932.

17. U.S. Bureau of Mines [Charles F. Jackson and John B. Knaebel], "Small Scale Placer Mining Methods," Information Cir-

cular 6611 (Washington: Government Printing Office, 1934, 5th rev.; orig. ed., 1932).

18. U.S. Bureau of Mines [Robert H. Ridgway], "Summarized Data of Gold Production," *Economic Paper* 6 (Washington: Government Printing Office, 1929), pp. 24–26; "Mine Inspector Issues Warning to Gold Miners," IDS, June 19,1932; Robert M. Bell, "Placer Gold Resources in Idaho," IDS, Aug. 7, 1932 and Aug. 14, 1932; "Boise River Fine Gold," IDS, Aug. 21, 1932; "Old Miners Claim Gold Still Hides in Hills of Wood River County," IDS, April 10, 1932; "Old Miners Still Search for Blue Bucket and Breyfogle Bonanza," IDS, May 22, 1932; H. A. Orchard, "Early Day Boise Basin Area Miners Carefully Explored Banks of Gravel in Search for Precious Bits of Ore," IDS, July 24, 1932.

19. C. McK. Laizure, "Elementary Placer Mining Methods and Gold Saving Devices," California Division of Mines, *Mining in California*, April 1932, p. 199.

20. "Idaho Gold Fields Respond to Boom in Placer Mining," IDS, April 16, 1932; "Salt Lake Gutter Yields $82 Gold," IDS, Aug. 10, 1932.

21. George Cantini, interview with C. W. Miller, Aug. 22, 1996.

22. Laizure, "Elementary Placer Mining Methods."

23. "Ancient Scales Used to Weigh Gold in Auburn," SB, June 28, 1932; "Gold Scales in Use in Oregon Village," IDS, July 11, 1932.

24. "Old Prospect Camp is Thriving Again," HDI, May 12, 1932.

25. Bradley papers, carton 3, folder 1932, BL.

26. Bradley, "An Echo of the Days of '49," E&MJ 135, no. 11, p. 49.

27. "Panning Gold," *Park County Republican*, Fairplay, Colo., July 1, 1931, repr. from LHD.

28. "Prospecting and the Unemployed," IDS, June 3, 1932; "Gold Rush of 1932 Begins with Boise Mining School," IDS, June 16, 1932; Campbell, "Mine Inspector Issues Warning," IDS, June 19, 1932; Bell, "Placer Gold Resources in Idaho," IDS, Aug. 7, 1932 and Aug. 14, 1932.

29. Otis E. Young, *Western Mining* (Norman: University of Oklahoma Press, 1970), pp. 102–18.

30. Duane A. Smith, "Life and Death Jostle One Another: Medicine in the Early Mining Camps," *1994 Annual of the Mining History Association*, pp. 45–50.

31. Bradley, "An Echo of the Days of '49," E&MJ 135, no. 11, p. 49.

32. Young, *Western Mining*, pp. 102–18; State of Arizona, Bureau of Geology and Mineral Technology [Eldred D. Wilson], "Gold Placers and Placering in Arizona," Bulletin 168 (Tucson: University of Arizona, 1961, 3d ed.; 1st ed.,1933), pp. 87–96; C. McK. Laizure, "Elementary Placer Mining and Gold Saving Devices," and H. H. Symons, "The Pan, Rocker, and Sluice Box," California Division of Mines, *Mining in California*, April 1932, pp. 112–205, and pp. 205–13.

33. "Prospecting Pan Shortage Is Good News," E&MJ 132, no. 2, p. 50; "Gold Pans in Demand," NYT, Nov. 12, 1933.

34. State of Arizona, Bureau of Geology and Mineral Technology [Eldred D. Wilson], "Gold Placers and Placering in Arizona," Bulletin 168 (Tucson: University of Arizona, 1961, 3d ed.; 1st ed., 1933), pp. 100–6; Robert M. Bell, "Placer Gold Resources in Idaho," IDS, Aug. 7, 1932 and Aug. 14, 1932.

35. "Amateur Prospectors Find the 'Gold in Them Thar Hills' is Hard to Catch," HDI, May 25, 1932.

36. "Increasing Gold Prospecting Embraces Entire World: Many Strikes Are Reported," E&MJ 134, no. 4, editorial pg.; "Gold Mining Best During Depression," *Los Angeles Times*, July 30, 1932; Bradley, "An Echo of the Days of '49," E&MJ 135, no. 11, p. 49.

37. U.S. Dept. of Commerce, Bureau of the Census, *Sixteenth Census, 1940, Mineral Industries*, vol. 1, pp. 337–59, 367–73 (comparative tables for 1929 and 1939).

38. "Children Strike Gold in Backyard Mining," *San Francisco Chronicle*, July 30, 1932.

39. "Grass Valley Miners Find Cavern of Gold," *San Francisco Chronicle*, Jan. 13, 1932; "Old Mother Lode Mine Gives Up $1300 Nugget," *San Francisco Chronicle*, Aug. 4, 1932.

40. "Amateur Prospector Wrests $3000 from Idaho Creek," NYT, Dec. 17, 1932; "Uninitiated Miners Leave Gold Fields to Old-Timers." IDS, Sept. 11, 1932.

41. A. H. Carhart, "Homemade Gold," *Saturday Evening Post*, Sept. 17, 1932, pp. 21, 31–32; S. G. Blythe, "The Argonauts of '32," *Saturday Evening Post*, Oct. 15, 1932, pp. 10–11, 33–34; F. R. Bechdolt, "Stampede, 1936 Model," *Saturday Evening Post*, Nov. 14, 1936, pp. 14–15, 53–54.

42. Carhart, "Homemade Gold."

43. Blythe, "Argonauts."

44. "Gold Diggers are Operating on All of the Creeks in the Sumpter Section," IDS, July 20, 1932; "Gold Rush in Oregon," LHD, June 26, 1934.

45. "200 in Sierra Gold Rush," NYT, July 14, 1932.

46. E. J. Webster, "Arizona Intrigued by Liquor and Gold," NYT, July 3, 1932.

47. "Denver Idle Learn to Pan Gold in South Platte River School," NYT, May 22, 1932; "Students Turn to Gold Mining," RMN, May 29, 1932.

48. "Stampede of Placer Miners Grows Apace in Northwest," IDS, June 6, 1932; "Placer School Attracts 1900," IDS, June 10, 1932; *Grubstaking the Palouse* (Pullman, Wash.: Washington State University Press, 1986), pp. 33–34; "Gold Rush of 1932," IDS, June 16, 1932; Calif. State Dept. of Education and Visual Education Dept. of the WPA, Adult Education Program, Gold Prospecting for Amateurs, (Los Angeles: Calif. State Education Dept., 1940), a complete curricula; "Success of Placer Mining," HDI, Aug. 7, 1932.

49. Albert S. Konselman, "Federal Grubstaking of Placer Mines," *Mining Journal*, Nov. 15, 1932, p. 5.

50. "Go Pan Some Gold," *San Diego Union*, Dec. 6, 1932.

51. Carl Wakefield, *San Francisco Examiner*, to Bradley, Apr. 20, 1934, carton 3, 1934 folder; Bradley diary, May 28, 1933, carton 3, BL.

52. W. H. Adams, secretary of Chamber of Commerce Radio Committee to Bradley, Mar. 28, 1935, carton 3, Chamber of Commerce File, Bradley Papers, BL.

53. "Search for Gold Calls 3,500 Into Gem State Mountains," IDS, June 27, 1932.

Chapter 2—Amateurs

1. "Swimming Pools Have Gold Linings," SB, May 29, 1934.

2. Tom White, "Old Trails of '49 Lure Miners of Today," NYT, June 11, 1933.

3. Stanley Zadach, "Placer Mining in San Gabriel Canyon," *Mining Journal*, June 30, 1933, p. 3.

4. Walter W. Bradley, "An Echo of the Days of '49," E&MJ 135, no. 11, pp. 494–96; State of Arizona, Bureau of Geology and Mineral Technology [Eldred D. Wilson], "Gold Placers and Placering in Arizona," Bulletin 168, (Tucson: University of Arizona, 1961, 3d ed.; 1st ed.,1933), pp. 102–7.

5. Safeway advertisement, LHD, Jan. 5, 1934; Frazier's Grocery Store advertisement, CC, July 23, 1931; Red and White Grocery advertisement and Arapahoe Food Store advertisement, CC, July 24, 1931; Safeway advertisement, MD, Apr. 1, 1934; series of advertisements, CdA, Jan. 12, 1934; series of advertisements, PC, May 13, 1932.

6. American Furniture Co., Broadhurst Shoe Co., and Denver Dry Goods Co. advertisements, DP, June 18, 1934; I. R. Johnson advertisement, CdA, Apr. 5, 1934; Case Men's Tailoring, advertisement, CdA, Jan. 3, 1934; Montgomery Ward's advertisement, CdA, Aug. 24, 1934.

7. Western Auto advertisement, PC, May 19, 1932, and June 9, 1932.

8. Gilbert C. Fite and Jim E. Reese, *An Economic History of the United States* (Boston: Houghton Mifflin, 1963), p. 583.

9. "California Plans Gold Hunt by 200,000," NYT, Mar. 14, 1933; "Creel Boosts Mine Industry," MD, Aug. 10, 1934.

10. "Seek Gold in Old Fields," NYT, Jan. 15, 1933.

11. "Old Denver Fire Engine Joins Colorado Gold Rush," NYT, Aug. 26, 1934; "Ancient Fire Engine May Snort Again in Latest Mining Craze," IDS, June 23, 1932.

12. "Placer Miner is Inventor of New Saver of Values," CC, July 21, 1931.

13. State of Arizona, Bureau of Geology and Mineral Technology

[Eldred D. Wilson], "Gold Placers and Placering in Arizona," Bulletin 168, (Tucson: University of Arizona, 1961, 3d ed.; 1st ed.,1933), pp. 107–11.

14. Ibid.

15. Duncan Aikman, "Again Bret Harte's Hills Stir to Gold," NYT, Oct. 8, 1933; George Cantini, interview with C. W. Miller, Aug. 22, 1996.

16. "Equipment News," E&MJ 134, no. 2, p. 86; advertisement in *Mines Magazine* 17 (Dec. 30, 1933), p. 7; "Gold Gravel Washing Devices Multiply," E&MJ 134, no. 4.

17. "Improved Gold Placer Machine Saves Water," E&MJ 134, no. 6, p. 258; advertisement, "Denver Gold Placer Unit," *Mining Journal*, May 30, 1932, p. 25.

18. Advertisements in *Literary Digest*, July 23, 1932, p. 1, and Aug. 27, 1932, p. 1; advertisement in NYT, Jan. 21, 1934; advertisements in DP, May 8, 1932, p. 20, July 19, 1934, p. 13; advertisement in *Saturday Evening Post*, Aug. 20, 1925, p. 51; Montgomery Ward advertisement, CdA, Oct. 3, 1934.

19. "Price of Gas in Boise Goes Up Four Cents," IDS, June 15, 1932; "Gasoline Price Drops One Cent," IDS, July 16, 1932.

20. "Equipment News," E&MJ 135, no. 7, p. 332.

21. "Industrial Progress," E&MJ 134, no. 12, p. 541.

22. Bradley, "An Echo of the Days of '49," E&MJ 135, no. 11, pp. 494–96; S. G. Blythe, "The Argonauts of '32," *Saturday Evening Post*, Oct. 15, 1932, pp. 10–11, 33–34.

23. "Small Yields," NYT, Feb. 22, 1932, p. 29; Frank H. Bartholomew, "10,000 Miners, Mostly Amateurs, Increase California Gold Output," YMS, July 7, 1932.

24. The preliminary report is Charles White Merrill, Charles O. Henderson, and O. E. Kiessling, *Small Scale Placer Mines as a Source of Gold Employment and Livelihood in 1935,* Report E2 (Philadelphia: U.S. Works Projects Administration, May 1937). The final report is Robinson Newcomb, Charles White Merrill, and R. L. Kiessling, *Employment and Income from Gold Placering by Hand Methods, 1935–1937*, Report E-14, (Philadelphia: U.S. Bureau of Mines and U.S. Works Projects Administration, June 1940).

25. Newcomb, Merrill, and Kiessling, *Employment and Income*, pp. vi-vii, 13.

26. Ibid., p. 4.

27. U.S. Dept. of the Interior, Census Office [Clarence King], *The United States Mining Laws* (Washington: Government Printing Office, 1885), pp. 331–33; William Downie, *Hunting for Gold* (Palo Alto, Calif.: American West Publishing Co., 1971; repr. of 1893 ed.), pp. 80–82.

28. Newcomb, Merrill, and Kiessling, *Employment and Income*, pp. 3–4.

29. Ibid., pp. 7–10, 39.

30. Ibid., pp. 9–10.

31. Ibid., pp. 7–8.

32. U.S. Bureau of Mines [C.E. Julian and F. W. Horton], *Mines of the Southern Mother Lode Region*, pt. I, Calaveras County, [Bulletin 413] (Washington: Government Printing Office, 1938), pp. 20–21.

33. Newcomb, Merrill, and Kiessling, *Employment and Income*, pp. 13, 20, 41, 52.

34. Ibid., pp. 14–16.

35. Ibid., pp. 47, 48, 54.

36. Ibid., p. 67.

37. Ibid., p. 137.

38. Ibid., pp. 30–34.

39. Ibid., pp. 53–54.

40. Ibid., p. 46.

41. Ibid., pp. 57–58.

42. Ibid., pp. 56, 62.

43. Ibid., pp. 58–60.

44. Ibid., pp. 69–72.

45. Ibid., pp. 72–77.

46. Ibid., pp. 78–89.

47. Merrill, Henderson, and Kiessling, *Small Scale Placer Mines*, p. 28.

48. Harry C. Chellson, "What Will It Cost to Work a Gold Placer of Medium Size?" E&MJ 135, no. 10, pp. 441–44.

49. "Gold," E&MJ 136, no. 1, pp. 28–29.

50. Harry C. Chellson, "United States," E&MJ 138, no. 2, pp. 73–75.

Chapter 3—Politics

1. Stanley L. Jones, *The Presidential Election of 1896* (Madison: University of Wisconsin Press, 1964), pp. 3–15.

2. Ibid., pp. 16–35. In 1892 the Populist party had become strong enough to run James B. Weaver for president. The Populist platform was based on free silver and other agrarian planks.

3. Ibid., pp. 238–39.

4. Ibid., pp. 332–51.

5. Hubert H. Bancroft, *Works of Hubert H. Bancroft* (New York: McGraw Hill, undated reprint of editions of 1883–1890), vol. 25, pp. 226–28; B. Levine, *Cities of Gold* (Colorado Springs: Century One Press, 1981), pp. 12–15; S. Holbrook, *Rocky Mountain Revolution* (New York: Holt, 1956), p. 72.

6. "Mining in the Mountain States," *Mining Journal* (Sept. 15, 1931): 32; "Bimetallism Urged by Bryan on Eve of Silver Parley," YMS (Feb. 14, 1932): 1.

7. Claude A. Jagger, "Plans to Help Silver Fail to Bolster Price," RMN, June 26, 1932.

8. Joan Hoff Wilson, *Herbert Hoover: Forgotten Progressive* (Boston: Little Brown, 1975), pp. 156–57; Herbert C. Hoover, *The Memoirs of Herbert Hoover: The Great Depression*, vol. 3 (New York: MacMillan, 1952), pp. 279–89, 390–407.

9. "Borah Advocates Silver as Issue in 1932 Campaign," IDS, June 9, 1932; "Idaho Group Booms Silver," IDS, June 13, 1932; "Free Silver," IDS, July 3, 1932.

10. James A. Haggerty "Roosevelt at Butte Pledges 'No Evasion On a Silver Parley'," NYT, Sept. 20, 1932.

11. Gold certificates were paper monetary notes issued by the government which could be exchanged for gold at the Treasury. Milton Friedman and Anna Schwartz, *A Monetary History of the U.S., 1867–1960* (Princeton: Princeton University Press, 1963), pp. 462–63; United States President, Executive Order 6102 and Executive Order 6111 (Washington: Government Printing Office, 1933).

12. U.S. Congress, House of Representatives, 73d Cong., 1st sess., Congressional Record, pp. 4546–48 (May 1933).

13. Ibid., p. 4563.

14. Ibid., Senate, p. 4929.

15. U.S. Congress, House of Representatives, 73d Congress, 2d sess., Congressional Record, pp. 963–68, 1016; Senate, Congressional Record, pp. 1484 (Jan. 1934).

16. Will Rogers, "What'll We Do About Silver?" SB, May 19, 1934.

17. U.S. Bureau of the Census, *Historical Statistics of the United States, Colonial Times to 1970* (Washington: Government Printing Office, 1975) pt. 1, p. 606.

18. "Chronology of New Deal Silver Legislation," E&MJ 140, pp. 78–79.

19. U.S. Congress, Senate, 73d Cong., 2d sess., *Congressional Record*, p. 1465 (Jan. 1934).

20. R. Moley, *The First New Deal* (New York: MacMillan, 1966), pp. 298–305.

21. U.S. Congress, House of Representatives, 73d Cong., 2d sess., *Congressional Record*, p. 107 (1934).

22. Ibid., p. 10580 (June 1934); "Will Consider Bill," SB, May 24, 1934.

23. U.S. Congress, Senate, 73d Congress, 2d sess., *Congressional Record*, pp. 10678–95.

24. "Europe Is Against Silver Experiment," SB, May 24, 1934.

25. U.S. Congress, Senate, 73d Cong., 2d sess., *Congressional Record*, pp. 10921–11060 (June 1934).

26. "Silver Depository," E&MJ 139, no. 7, p. 74; "United States Bullion Depository" (Fort Knox, Ky.: Patton Museum of Cavalry and Armour, n.d.), pp. 2, 5.

27. Roosevelt, Public Papers, vol. 3, item 89, pp. 253–56.

28. Rogers, "What'll We Do About Silver?" SB, May 19, 1934.

29. "Senate Orators Will Launch Nationwide Drive for Free Silver," and "Federal Silver Purchases Under New Act," DP, June 21, 1934; "News From Washington," E&MJ 140, no. 7, p. 68.

30. "Mine Boom in the West," NYT, Oct. 25, 1934.

31. "Assessment Exemption Bill Passed," E&MJ 134, no. 2, p. 86; "Mining Claims and the New Deal," E&MJ 134, no. 5, p. 183; "Annual Assessment Work on Mining Claims," E&MJ 135 no. 4, p. 146; A. H. Hubbell, "Again, the Question of Assessment Work," E&MJ 140, no. 3, pp. 38–40; "Assessment Work Suspensions: A Hardy Annual," E&MJ 136, no. 6, p. 266.

32. "News From Washington," E&MJ 138, no. 2, pp. 105–6.

33. Robert S. McElvaine, *The Great Depression* (New York: Times Books, 1984), pp. 158–61.

34. "Nonferrous Metal Codes Pour In At Washington," and "Mining More Active as NRA Rulings Become Effective," E&MJ 134, no. 9, pp. 356–63, 389; "Study the Proposed National Mineral Policy," and "NRA and Mining Industries," E&MJ 136, no. 4, pp. 161–62; "Supreme Court Holds NRA Codes Invalid," E&MJ 136, no. 6, p. 265.

35. McElvaine, *The Great Depression*, pp. 258–61; "Federal Legislation Affects Mining Industry," E&MJ 136, no. 9, pp. 433–34; H. Howard Meyers, *Labor Law* (Cincinnati: Southwest Publishing, 4th ed., 1968), p. 449; "Mediation Effects Settlement of Major Labor Dispute in Mining Industry," E&MJ 135, pp. 436–37.

36. H. D. Keiser, "Silicosis Compensation," E&MJ 135, no. 1, p. 34.

37. "News From Washington," E&MJ 135, no. 10, p. 469; "Approved Mining Loans by RFC," E&MJ 139, no. 9, p. 73.

38. "Increased Price Put on Gold Adds to Interest in Mining," MD, Apr. 13, 1934, p. 12.

Chapter 4—Professionals

1. Two excellent practical mining handbooks originally published in the 1930s and revised in 1941 reflect mining techniques developed during the Depression decade: Robert Peele, *Mining Engineer Handbook*, 3d ed. (New York: John Wiley, 1941), discusses explosives on pp. 4-17 to 4-21, hand drilling on pp. 5-7, mucking on pp. 6-15, timbering on pp. 6-21 to 6-29, power drilling on pp. 10-92 to 10-99, and hole patterns on pp. 10-99 to 10-101; Robert S. Lewis, *Elements of Mining*, 2d ed. (New York: John Wiley, 1941) describes explosives including black powder, pp. 96–119, drilling, pp. 132–42, mucking, p. 174, and timbering, pp. 272–82.

2. Chapin Hall, "Gold Boom Stirs Southern California," NYT, Nov. 26, 1933.

3. "Gold Strike in Idaho," ibid., July 10, 1932; "Mine at Pearl Starts Up Mill," IDS, Sept. 3, 1932.

4. "High Price of Gold Revives Atlanta, Silver City Camps," IDS, July 22, 1932; "Miner Reports Gold Discovery," IDS, July 7, 1932; "Gold Properties Boon to Elk City," CdA, Jan. 18, 1934; "Mining Companies Take Out Articles of Incorporation," IDS, Aug. 16, 1932.

5. "Blind Nevada Miner Strikes Gold," SB, June 16, 1931; "Mine Idle for 60 Years to Operate Again," SB, June 30, 1931.

6. "Gold Strike Reported," IDS, June 22, 1932; "Striking of Vein Precipitates Rush to Alaskan Fields," IDS, July 1, 1932; "Two Alaskans Find Biggest Ledge of Gold," IDS, June 28, 1932.

7. "Gold Mining Activity Shows Steady Gain Thru Colorado," RMN, June 26, 1932.

8. "Colorado Gold Rush Started by Strike," NYT, May 14, 1933; "Colorado Rush Led by Negro Prospector," *Newsweek*, July 15, 1933, p. 6.

9. "Alma District's Gold Mines Write Gratifying Story," *Park County Republican and Fairplay Flume*, Jan. 1, 1932; "Alma Sends Out Longest Ore Train in Camp's History," *Park County Republican and Fairplay Flume*, Jan. 15, 1932; "Long Ore Trains Prove Alma District Mineral Richness," *Park County Republican and Fairplay Flume*, Mar. 4, 1932; "More Ore Than 3 Engines Could

Draw Left Alma Tues.," *Park County Republican and Fairplay Flume,* April 22, 1932; "Over 100 Cars of Gold Being Shipped to Leadville Smelter Each Month," *Alma Mining Record,* June 28, 1935; "Alma Mines Ship 134 Cars in June," *Park County Republican and Fairplay Flume,* July 8, 1932.

10. "Slot Machine Thieves Do Some Bold and Novel Work in County," *Park County Republican and Fairplay Flume,* June 3, 1932.

11. "Fairplay to Enjoy Picture Show Again," *Park County Republican and Fairplay Flume,* Jan. 29, 1932, p. 1.

12. A. H. Carhart, "Homemade Gold," *Saturday Evening Post,* Sept. 17, 1932, pp. 21, 31–32; F. Briscoe, "Aspects of Local Mining State as Seen by a Newcomer," *Saturday Evening Post,* Jan. 1, 1932; Charles W. Henderson, "Colorado, Storehouse of Varied Mineral Wealth," E&MJ 136, no. 7, pp. 369–71.

13. The author discussed the Earps in *Stake Your Claim!* (Tucson: Westernlore Press, 1991), pp. 144–46.

14. Edwin J. Webster, "Gold Fever Strikes Arizona Once More," NYT, May 22, 1932; "Increased Activity in Mining District," YMS, Apr. 14, 1932.

15. "Many Prospectors Reported Working in Maricopa Hills," YMS, June 18, 1932.

16. W. F. Dunn, "Yuma County Mining News," *Yuma County Record,* Mar. 24, 1933.

17. "New Gold Strike Reported in Altar Valley of Sonora," YMS, Apr. 24, 1932; "Rich Gold Strike Reported in Mexico," IDS, Apr. 19, 1932.

18. "Mexico," E&MJ 133, no. 2, p. 63; Ernest Schürer and Philip Jenkins, eds., *B. Traven Life and Work* (Univ. Park: Penn State University Press, 1987), pp. 1–11.

19. "New Gold Finds Lure Thousands to Arctic Area," IDS, Apr. 17, 1932; "Gold Hunters Rush to North," IDS, Apr. 23, 1932.

20. "Trends and Developments in the Industry," E&MJ 134, no. 5, p. 216; "Prospectors Use Washing Machines for Washing Gold," NYT, Aug. 26, 1935.

21. G. A. Schroter, "A Geologist Visits the Mohave Mining District," E&MJ 136, no. 4, pp. 185–88; "Silver Queen Goes on Gold Standard," NYT, Dec. 9, 1934.

22. "California Gold Rush On," NYT, Dec. 6, 1934; John Huttl, "Activity Spurred in Camps of Southern California," E&MJ 136, no. 7, pp. 343–46.

23. Frederick R. Bechdolt, "Stampede, 1936 Model," *Saturday Evening Post*, Nov. 14, 1936, pp. 14–15, 53–56.

24. Roy Hardy, "The Getchell Mine, New Gold Producer of Nevada," E&MJ 139, no. 11, p. 29.

25. Marshall Sprague, *Money Mountain* (Boston: Little Brown, 1953) addresses the entire historic development of Cripple Creek; C. W. Henderson, "Colorado, Storehouse of Varied Mineral Wealth," E&MJ 136, no 7, pp. 369–71; G. F. Loughlin, "Cripple Creek Today," E&MJ, no. 8, pp. 372–75.

26. F. W. Bruington, "The New Cripple Creek Mill," *Mines Magazine*, vol. 25, pp. 16, 23; John Huttl, "Colorado Camps Active," E&MJ 135, no. 2, pp. 74–76; "Cripple Creek Discards Crutches in Gold Boom," *NYT*, Oct. 29, 1934; M. I. Singer, "Drainage for Cripple Creek District," E&MJ 140, no. 12, pp. 34–36; "Colorado," E&MJ 138, no. 5, p. 229.

27. "First Annual Donkey Derby Sweepstakes Gold Rush, Aug. 15–16," CC, July 18, 1931; "35 Donkeys Entered in Races Today," CC, Aug. 15, 1931; "Cripple Creek's Donkey Derby Brings Thousands to Gold Camp," CC, Aug. 17, 1931, p. 1.

28. Fred M. Miller, "Prosperity Rules in Grass Valley and Nevada City," E&MJ, vol. 135, no. 11, pp. 511–15.; John Huttl, "Grass Valley Gold Mines Hold Their Place," ibid., no. 12, pp. 617–18.

29. "Idle Mines in Forbestown District, California, to Be Rehabilitated," E&MJ. 136, no. 9, p. 464.

30. The entire Apr. 13, 1934, issue of MD was devoted to revival of activity; "Gold Miners' Club Founded," MD, Feb. 23, 1934, p. 1.

31. Karen Goudy, "Life in a Boom Town—Oatman, Arizona," in J. M. Cantry and M. N. Greeley, *History of Mining in Arizona* (Tucson: Mining Club of the Southwest Foundation, 1987), pp. 153–76; "Oatman Mines to Cooperate," E&MJ, vol. 131, no. 2, p. 83. For

the court cases see C. W. Miller, *Stake Your Claim!*, p. 159. Basic background of the complex apex rule appears on pp. 48–51.

32. "Gold in Black Hills Again Lures Miners," NYT, Nov. 7, 1933.

33. "New Gold Mining Activities Loom in Famous Maryville Camp," HDI, Aug. 21, 1932; "Paymaster Mine to Receive Machinery," HDI, Sept. 8, 1932; "Rich Gold Vein in Vosburg Mine Near Winston," HDI, Sept. 24, 1932; "Ophir Creek Mining Area Active Again," HDI, July 3, 1932.

34. "Sutro Tunnel Opens New Ore in Crown Point Mine," E&MJ 131, no. 9, p. 431; George Young, "Mountain Copper Co. Mine," E&MJ, no. 12, pp. 578–80; John Burgess, "Mining Gold on Carson Hill," E&MJ 136, no. 3, p. 111.

35. "Placer Mining in the Murray Gold Belt, Idaho, Follows Testing," E&MJ, no. 9, p. 465–66.

36. "Dredging Increases in California," E&MJ 135, no. 7, p. 290; C.M. Romanowitz and George Young, "Gold Dredging Receives New Impetus," E&MJ, no. 11, pp. 486–90; C. M. Romanowitz "Dredging," E&MJ 142, no. 8, p. 115.

37. "California Gold Continues to Enrich the Nation," E&MJ 135, no. 11, pp. 481–85; U. S. Bureau of Mines (C. E. Julian and F. W. Horton), *Southern Mother Lode Region*, pt. 1, Calaveras County, pp. 17, 20–22.

38. C. M. Romanowitz and George Young, "$35 Gold Stimulates the Dredge Designer's Ingenuity," E&MJ 135, no. 8, pp. 338–41.

39. John Huttl, "Arro Seco's New Dredge," E&MJ 136, no. 10, pp. 494–95.

40. "Equipment News," E&MJ 135, no. 7, p. 332.

41. John Huttl, "Natoma's Newest Dredge Has Novel Points of Design," E&MJ 136, no. 6, p. 270.

42. "California," E&MJ 139 no. 1, p. 70; Cyril Thomas, "When a Gold Dredge Capsizes," E&MJ 138, no. 6, p. 279; "California," *Mining Journal*, Mar. 15, 1941, p. 20, May 15, 1941, p. 21.

43. "Dragline and Stacker Scow," E&MJ 135, no. 8, p. 365; "Gold Mining Operations Increase in Old and New Areas," E&MJ 135, no. 7, pp. 321–24; H. C. Chellson, "U.S. Mining Revives," E&MJ

137, no. 2, pp. 73–74, 78–79; "Old Placer Area in Madison County to Be Worked Again," HDI, Aug. 7, 1932.

44. "Value of Idaho Mine Output Is Greater in 1933," CdA, Jan. 12, 1934.

45. State of Arizona, Bureau of Geology and Mineral Technology [Eldred D. Wilson], "Gold Placers and Placering in Arizona," Bulletin 168 (Tucson: University of Arizona, 1961, 3d ed.; 1st ed.,1933), pp. 38–43, 48–53.

46. Frank A. Kennedy, "Where Jigs Replaced Sluice Boxes," E&MJ 139, no. 7, pp. 50–54.

47. Clark Spence, *The Northern Gold Fleet* (Urbana: University of Illinois Press, 1996), pp. 110, 205.

48. Ibid., pp. 94–95.

49. "Moving a Gold Dredge Overland," E&MJ 132, no. 1, pp. 11–12; "Nome, Famous Gold Town Again on Front Page," CdA, Sept. 18, 1934, p. 1.

50. "Use Gold Dust for Money," NYT, Mar. 13, 1933.

51. Alaska Commissioner of Mines [B. D. Stewart], *Report, 1934–1936* (Juneau: Territory of Alaska, 1937), pp. 15, 18; Alaska Commissioner of Mines [B. D. Stewart], *Report, 1939–1940* (Juneau: Territory of Alaska, 1941) pp. 40, 45, 49, 52. Figures cited by Spence in *The Northern Gold Fleet*, p. 112, which were themselves taken from several other contemporary technical publications, are very close to those of the Commissioner of Mines until 1940, when Spence cited only 48 dredges in operation.

52. U.S. Bureau of the Census, *Historical Statistics, Colonial Times to 1970*, vol. 1 (Washington: Government Printing Office, 1975), p. 24.

53. Huttl, "Colorado Camps Active," pp. 74–76.

54. H. W. C. Prommel, "Colorado Attracts Another Large Bucket Dredge," E&MJ, 142, no. 10, pp. 35–37; Colorado Geological Survey [John and Halka Chronic], *Prairie, Peak, and Plateau: A Guide to the Geology of Colorado, Bulletin 32* (Denver: Colorado Geological Survey, 1972), pp. 83–85.

55. Since *Mines* is produced by the Colorado School of Mines, it

reported graduations annually as follows: June 1932, p. 21, June 1932, p. 6, June 1933, p. 9, June 1934, p. 13, June 1935, pp. 16–17, June 1936, pp. 14–16, June 1937, pp. 12–13, 26, June 1938, p. 273, June 1939, p. 334, June 1940, p. 321, June 1941, p. 289.

56. U.S. Bureau of the Census, *Historical Statistics*, pp. 383, 386.

57. "State to Help Small Miners," IDS, Apr. 6, 1932.

58. Temple Crane to Walter Bradley, Aug. 30, 1934, Bradley Papers, BL; "Gold Awarded Fair Premium," MD, Sept. 13, 1934; "Piece of Gold to Represent Idaho," IDS, Aug. 20, 1932.

Chapter 5—Silver and Spin Offs

1. U.S. Bureau of the Census, *Historical Statistics of the United States, Colonial Times to 1970* (Washington: Government Printing Office, 1975) pt. 1, pp. 602, 606.

2. "Growth of Gold Mining," AR, June 25, 1934.

3. "Revival Seen for Old Gold Camp," and "Burro Pack Train Brings Ore," *Bingham Bulletin*, June 15, 1934; "New Life Seen in Ghost Town," CdA, July 6, 1934.

4. "Bonanza Comstock Values Come to Light in Ophir Mine," *Mining Journal*, Oct. 30, 1933.

5. "Leadville Grand Total $557,254,251.98," LHD, Jan. 1, 1936.

6. "Population of Leadville Shows Encouraging Gain," LHD, June 7, 1934.

7. "Summary of Leadville Events for Prior Year," LHD, Jan. 1, 1936; Duane A. Smith, *Horace Tabor, His Life and the Legend*, (Boulder: Colorado Associated University Press, 1973), p. 367 (discussion in endnote).

8. Edward Blair, *Leadville: Colorado's Magic City* (Boulder: Pruett Publishers, 1980), pp. 116–18, 234–35.

9. Roger McGrath, *Gunfighters, Highwaymen, and Vigilantes* (Berkeley: Univ. of Calif. Press, 1984), p. 251.

10. Articles from *Telluride Journal*, "35 Carloads of Concentrates Shipt in July," Aug. 3, 1935; "Telluride Schools Increase of 31% over Previous Year," Nov. 10, 1934; "Telluride Scene of Substantial

Mining Activity," Dec. 6, 1934; "Black Bear Mine Is Sold For a Million Dollars," Dec. 23, 1934; "400 Tons of Old Tailings Milled Daily," Sept. 15, 1934.

11. U.S. Department of the Interior, "Red Arrow Gold Discovery in the La Plata Mountains, Colorado," Memorandum For Press, COSH C4:111; "Prospector Sues For Interest in Rich Colorado Gold Mine," DP, June 23, 1934.

12. Robert A. Heinlein, personal interview with the author, July 1963; Leon Stover, *Robert A. Heinlein* (Boston: Twayne Publishers, 1987), p. 18.

13. "Placer Mining in the Murray Gold Belt, Idaho, Follows Testing," E&MJ 136, no. 9, p. 465–66.

14. Richard D. Magnuson, *Coeur d'Alene Diary* (Portland: Metropolitan Press, 1968), pp. 216–42.

15. V. Jensen, *Heritage of Conflict* (Ithaca: Cornell Univ. Press, 1950), pp. 74–87; William S. Greever, *Bonanza West* (Moscow: University of Idaho Press, 1963), pp. 279–82.

16. *Bonanza West*, pp. 282–85; Walter Lord, *The Good Years* (New York: Harper Bros., 1960), pp. 140–67.

17. Morris Wright, *It Takes More Than Guns* (Denver: International Union of Mine, Mill, and Smelter Workers, 1944), pp. 5–9. Note that this short publication, the union's sponsored history, takes its title from the lyrics of "The Ballad of Joe Hill," the folk song which championed labor and portrayed Hill as a martyr to the cause.

18. Ibid., pp. 25–27; Frank A. Crampton, *Deep Enough* (Norman: University of Oklahoma Press, 1982 repr. of 1956 ed.) pp. 238–40.

19. "Union Miners Gain Decision," CdA, June 4, 1934; "Union Miners Win Election," CdA, June 9, 1934; Wright, *More than Guns*, p. 38.

20. "Silver-Lead, Zinc Prices Stimulate Coeur d'Alene Wage Increase," E&MJ 136, no. 6, pp. 296–98; "Idaho," E&MJ 138, no. 2, p. 204.

21. "Mediators Work on Mining Strike," CdA, Aug. 8, 1934; "Labor and Anaconda Officials in Deadlock at Butte," E&MJ 135, p. 280.

22. "Mediation Effects Settlement of Major Labor Dispute," E&MJ 135, pp. 436–37; "Montana Copper Strike Is Ended," CdA, Sept. 18, 1934.

23. "Sunshine Declares $240,000 Dividend," CdA, June 13, 1934; "Sunshine to Hit 2300 Foot Level," CdA, July 5, 1934; "Prove Ore Body," CdA, Nov. 20, 1934.

24. "Places Order for Firework Display," CdA, June 13, 1934; "New Ward's Store Open Tomorrow," CdA, Aug. 24, 1934; advertisement, "Bell's Food Store, Grand Opening," CdA, Feb. 16, 1934; advertisement, "New Red and White, Grand Opening," CdA, Nov. 26, 1934.

25. U.S. Department of Commerce, Bureau of the Census (Washington: Government Printing Office, 1942–44), *Population*, vol. I, pp. 91, 627, 1084, vol. II, pt. 2, pp. 428–30, 467; Census, *Historical Statistics*, pp. 28–34.

26. "Park City District in Utah Becoming More Active as Large Mine Reopens," E&MJ 136, no. 12, pp. 620–21; Allan Kent Powell, ed., *Utah History Encyclopedia* (Salt Lake City: University of Utah Press, 1994).

27. "Welcome to Tombstone," and "Boothill," TE, Jan. 5, 1933; "Many Tourists Are Pleased with Our Sights and History," TE, April 13, 1933; "Work at ASARCO Unit Progresses Through Mine," TE, June 22, 1933; "Mining!" TE, Nov. 2, 1933.

28. "42 Cars of Ore in October, Largest Shipment in More Than 10 Years," TE, Nov. 1, 1934; "Trends and Developments in the Industry," E&MJ 134, no. 5, p. 216; "Arizona," E&MJ, no. 10, p. 494.

29. "Survey of Our Mining District Shows Increase in Activity," TE, Mar. 8, 1934; "Down They Go with Gold in the Bottom of Holes," TE, Oct. 11, 1934; "More than 300 Working at Mining Here," TE, June 28, 1934; advertisement, Russ House, TE, Aug. 9, 1934; U.S. Department of Commerce, Census, *Population*, vol. I (1940), p. 91.

30. "Mine, Smelter to Shut Down," PC, May 7, 1932; "Magma to Shut Down July 1," PC, May 27, 1932; "Inspiration Mine Closed, Leaving 500 Jobless," YMS, May 8, 1932; U.S. Bureau of the Census, *Census of Mines*, 1939 (Washington: Government Printing Office, 1944), pp. 381–419.

31. U.S. Bureau of the Census, *Historical Statistics*, p. 602.

32. "New York Stock Exchange," AR, Sept. 17, 1929 and Sept. 17, 1932; "Anaconda Reports Loss," IDS, April 14, 1932.

33. "Commissioner Makes Huge Cut Valuation Mining Property," YMS, July 12, 1932.

34. "Mormon Church Backs Move for Copper Tariff," YMS, April 16, 1932. The background of Mormon antagonism to mining is in James F. Varley, *Brigham and the Brigadier* (Tucson: Westernlore Press, 1989), pp. 155–56, 178–79.

35. Connor received his brigadier general's star for carrying forward the largest Indian massacre in the history of the West when he attacked an encampment of Northwestern Shoshoni at dawn on the bitter-cold morning of January 29, 1863, at Bear River, near Franklin, Idaho, killing 250 men, women, and children. See Brigham D. Madsen, *Glory Hunter: Patrick Edward Connor* (Salt Lake City: University of Utah Press, 1990).

36. "New York Stock Exchange," AR, June 17, 1934 and Sept. 17, 1935; U.S. Bureau of the Census, *Historical Statistics*, p. 602.

37. Lynn R. Bailey, *Bisbee: Queen of the Copper Camps* (Tucson: Westernlore Press, 1983), pp. 135–38; H.C. Parmlee, "A Century of Progress," E&MJ 134, no. 7, pp. 290–93.

38. "Upward Swing of Metal Prices," E&MJ 138, no. 1, p. 1; John B. Huttl, "High Price Helps California Quicksilver," E&MJ 138, no. 1, p. 3.

39. All the railroad discussion is from Colorado Railroad Museum, *Colorado Rail Annual No. 18, Railroads in the Rockies a Half Century Ago* (Golden: Colorado Railroad Museum, 1990), p. 14, map of the West in appendix.

40. Isaac F. Marcosson, *Metal Magic: The Story of ASARCO* (New York: Farrar, Straus and Co., 1949), pp. 146–52.

41. Casper A. Nelson, "Smelters," in *Midvale History, 1851–1979*, edited by Maurine C. Jensen (N.p.: n.p., n.d.), p. 233; "Concentration and Lead Smelting at Midvale, Utah," E&MJ 134, no. 6, pp. 248–49.

42. Stock prices from "New York Stock Exchange," AR, Sept. 17, 1929, Sept. 17, 1932, Sept. 17, 1933, and June 17, 1934.

43. All these descriptions are from typical advertisements in E&MJ, 1937 through 1941, as follows: 139, no. 1, p. 69; 139, no. 3, p. 75; 139, no. 4, pp. 67, 79; 139, no. 8, p. 100; 142, no. 2, p. 131; 142, no. 3, pp. 80–83; 142, no. 4, p. 85.

44. U.S. Census, 1940, *Mineral Industries, 1939* (Washington: Government Printing Office, 1944) pp. 342–60.

45. U.S. Census, 1940, *Mineral Industries, 1939*, pp. 345–50; "Gold Output Gained in Alaska," NYT, July 6, 1931; "Alaska Now Feels Depression Blight," NYT, Jan. 1, 1933.

46. U.S. Census, 1940, *Mineral Industries 1939*, pp. 361–72.

Chapter 6—Giants' Return

1. Philip Ross May, *Origins of Hydraulic Mining in California* (Oakland: Holmes Book Co., 1970), pp. 40, 45; Otis E. Young, *Western Mining* (Norman: University of Oklahoma Press, 1970), pp. 125–31.

2. Charles Howard Shinn, *Mining Camps: A Study in American Frontier Government* (New York: Alfred A. Knopf, 1948, repr. of 1884 pbl.) pp. 255–56; Leroy A. Palmer, "Hydraulic Mining Looks Up in California," E&MJ 1, no. 10, pp. 29–33; *Opinions of Lorenzo Sawyer*, Circuit Judge, and Matthew P. Deady, District Judge, in the case of *Edwards Woodruff v. North Bloomfield Gravel Mining Co., et al.*, Jan. 7, 1884 (published as a separate volume but no place or publisher cited), pp. 4, 53.

3. *Opinions of Lorenzo Sawyer*, pp. 2, 9, 12; Rowland Egenhoff, "The Hydraulic Mining Situation in California," transcript of speech given before the American Society of Civil Engineers, Jan. 28, 1931, at Sacramento, pp. 1–4, Bancroft Library, Berkeley.

4. James D. Stewart, "Hydraulic Mining Again Interesting to Capital," E&MJ 135, no. 11, pp. 491–93; *U.S. Army Annual Report of the Chief of Engineers*, vol. 2 (Washington: Government Printing Office, 1957), pp. 1891–1905; Egenhoff, "Hydraulic Mining Situation," p. 5.

5. Palmer, "Hydraulic Mining," pp. 29–33; Stewart, "Hydraulic Mining," pp. 491–93; "Report of Gov. Rolph's Committee of 15 and a Review of Insurance and Mining Bills Before the State Legis-

lature," BL, carton 1, 1933 folder; "An Untouched Billion of California Gold," *California Mining Journal 2*, no. 2, pp. 2, 10, 12.

6. "Gold Mining Revival Planned in California," NYT, July 3, 1932.

7. Stewart, "Hydraulic Mining," "Placer Mining Bill Is Signed Over Protests," SB, June 13, 1933; "Debris Commission to Get Mining Permit," SU, May 5, 1934, p. 11; "Debris Dams Must Not Be Makeshifts," *Grass Valley Union*, Dec. 3, 1932.

8. "Report of Gov. Rolph's Committee," James D. Stewart to W. H. Taylor Co., Oct. 17, 1933, BL, carton 3, file 1933.

9. "Hydraulic Property Directed by Woman," MD, Apr. 13, 1934; "Unique Mining Plan Is to Be Used," SB, May 17, 1934.

10. U.S. Congress, *Statutes at Large of the United States*, 73rd Congress, 2nd Session (Washington: Government Printing Office, 1935), Public Law 425, p. 1118.

11. Stewart, "Hydraulic Mining," pp. 491–93; Walter W. Bradley, *Present Status of Hydraulic Mine Debris Disposal in California* (New York: American Institute of Mining Engineers, 1936), pp. 6–9.

12. The Saywer Decision affected only rivers in central California, not rivers in the northwest corner of the state in California's other major gold area.

13. Advertisement for Joshua Hendry Iron Works, E&MJ 139, no. 4, p. 82; Robert E. Bell, "Placer Gold Resources in Idaho," IDS, Aug. 7, 1932.

14. "California Dredge Owners Get Break on Top Soil Bill," *Mining Journal* (Apr. 30, 1935): 5; "California," E&MJ 136, no. 12, p. 626; Bradley to Editor, *San Francisco News*, Jan. 26, 1935, BL, carton 3, folder 1935.

15. Palmer, "Hydraulic Mining," pp. 29–33.

16. Stewart to Bradley, Feb. 13, 1935, BL, carton 3, folder 1935.

17. Englebright to Bradley, Aug. 9, 1935, BL, carton 3, folder 1935; Palmer, "Hydraulic Mining," pp. 29–33; Walter W. Bradley, "Dams for Hydraulic Mining Debris," *California Journal of Mines and Geology 31*, no. 3, pp. 345–67.

18. Palmer, "Hydraulic Mining," pp. 29–33.

19. *U.S. Army Annual Report*, pp. 1891–1905.

20. "California," *Mining Journal* (July 15, 1940): 22; (Aug. 30, 1940): 18; (Jan. 15, 1941): 16.

21. Advertisement, E&MJ 139, no. 4, p. 82.

22. "California," *Mining Journal* (June 30, 1940): 19; (July 15, 1940): 24; (Nov. 15, 1940): 24–25; (Jan. 15, 1941): 15; (Apr. 15, 1941): 21.

23. J. M. Erhorn, "Hydraulicking for Gold at Poverty Hill," E&MJ 139, no. 11, pp. 65–68; "Placer Operations Add to Domestic Gold Output," E&MJ 147, no. 6, pp. 101–2; "California," E&MJ 147, no. 10, p. 98; D. C. Demarest, "The Mother Lode Is Not Dead," E&MJ 152, no. 3, pp. 63–67.

24. "Injunction Served on Hydraulic Mine," SB, June 30, 1931.

25. "California," *Mining Journal* (June 30, 1940): 19; (July 15, 1940): 22; (Aug. 15, 1940): 20; (Aug. 30, 1940): 18; (Nov. 15, 1940): 24; (Dec. 30, 1940): 17.

26. *U.S. Army Annual Report*, pp. 1891–1905; *U.S. Army Annual Report of the Chief of Engineers*, vol. 2 (Washington: Government Printing Office, 1963), pp. 2109–11.

27. Palmer, "Hydraulic Mining," pp. 29–33; Robert L. Kelley, *Gold vs. Grain* (Glendale, California: Arthur H. Clark, 1959), pp. 271–75.

28. For example, see Walton Bean, *California: An Interpretive History* (New York: McGraw-Hill, 1968), p. 278, Andrew F. Rolle, *California: A History* (New York: Thomas Y. Crowell, 1969), pp. 483, 508, and James D. Hart, *A Companion to California* (Berkeley: University of California Press, 1987), which make no mention of hydraulic mining at all.

Chapter 7—Aftermath

1. "Reflections," and "News of the Industry," E&MJ 143, no. 11, pp. 43–44, 77; "Reflections from Washington," E&MJ 143, no. 12, pp. 45–46.

2. Herbert Hoover, *The Memoirs of Herbert Hoover: The Great Depression, 1929–1941*, vol. 3 (New York: MacMillan, 1952), pp. 390–401.

3. Arthur M. Schlesinger, *The Coming of the New Deal* (Boston: Little Brown, 1957), pp. 244–52.

4. Frank Friedel, *Franklin D. Roosevelt: Rendezvous with Destiny* (Boston: Little Brown, 1990), p. 139.

5. Milton Friedman, *Money Mischief* (New York: Harcourt, Brace, and Jovanovich, 1992), pp. 147–69; Kurt R. Leube, ed., *The Essence of Friedman* (Palo Alto, Calif.: Hoover Institution Press, 1987), pp. 329–30, 344.

6. "Treasury Outlining Silver Bill," AR, June 22, 1934, p. 1.

7. Roosevelt, *The Public Papers of Franklin D. Roosevelt*, (New York: Random House, 1938), vol. 3, 1934, item 89, pp. 253–56.

8. "Not More Gold but Figures," AR, June 22, 1934; "Silver Hocus Pocus?" *Sacramento Union*, May 25, 1934; "FDR Offers Plan for U.S. Silver Buying," CdA, May 22, 1934.

9. "Copper Mines Add 1000 to Payroll: Miami, Ajo, Scenes of Renewal in Activity; Silver is Aid," AR, June 30, 1934.

10. Ray Allen Billington, *Westward Expansion* (New York: MacMillan, 1967; 4th ed.), pp. 766–67 (a bibliographic essay on the "safety valve").

11. "And They Are Bold Who Woo the Gold," IDS, Sept. 25, 1932.

Appendix—Silver, Gold, and Currency

1. The basic formula, P=M/T (where P stands for prices, M stands for the total money supply in an economically identifiable unit, and T stands for total goods and services offered in the economy), expresses the essence of monetarist economics—an increase in the money supply will make P, prices, a higher number. Joan Hoff Wilson, *Herbert Hoover: Forgotten Progressive* (Boston: Little Brown), pp. 156–57.

2. Milton Friedman and Anna Schwartz, *A Monetary History of the United States, 1867–1960* (Princeton: Princeton Univ. Press, 1963), pp. 462–63.

3. Franklin D. Roosevelt, *Complete Press Conferences of Franklin D. Roosevelt, 1933* (New York: DaCampo Press, 1972) vol. 1, pp.

160–61; Roosevelt, *Public Papers*, vol. 3, pp. 40–54, 67–76 (items 8, 9, and 16).

4. Friedman and Schwartz, *Monetary History*, pp. 470, 485.

5. Ibid., pp. 465–66.

6. Ibid., pp. 434–37.

7. Frank Friedel, *Franklin D. Roosevelt: Launching the New Deal* (Boston: Little Brown, 1973), p. 324.

8. Friedman and Schwartz, *Monetary History*, p. 484. See also Milton Friedman, *Monetary Mischief* (New York: Harcourt Brace, & Jovanovich, 1992), pp. 162–64, which unequivocally describes the situation as "bizarre."

Index